QUICK THINKING ON YOUR FEET

VALERIE PIERCE

D1643257

MERCIER PRESS
WHAT YOU NEED TO READ

MERCIER PRESS
CORK
WWW.MERCIERPRESS.IE

TRADE ENQUIRIES TO COLUMBA MERCIER DISTRIBUTION,
55A SPRUCE AVENUE, STILLORGAN INDUSTRIAL PARK, BLACKROCK,
DUBLIN

ISBN: 978 1 85635 409 7

10 9 8 7 6 5

Logo & book cover designed by House of Design. See website:
www.houseofdesign.com

Printed and bound in the EU.

CONTENTS

IN MEMORY OF LAURENCE
WHOSE SILENT STRENGTH SAID IT ALL

Welcome

> *Humans are full of convictions, animated by the desire to convince*
> Philippe Breton, *La Parole Manipulée*

About you

For all those readers like myself, who have what the French call an excellent *esprit d'escalier* – staircase wit – this book is for you.

'Staircase wit' happens like this. You want to persuade others you have a great idea. You want to argue clearly, without emotion, and to the point. But then it doesn't happen and later you think of all the wonderful things you could have said. *Staircase wit is the incredible ability to come up with all those devastating rejoinders just as we're going up the stairs to bed that night ... when it's too late.*

Of course, it shouldn't happen like that, and if you can learn to think quickly on your feet, *at the time you need to*, it won't. A lot of the time the inability to get what you want is not because you cannot argue well enough, it is because you have been manipulated to lose your train of thought.

Awareness

When we enter into discussion, we hope to meet with clear, persuasive argument. Alas, far too often we are bombarded by false and sometimes manipulative reasoning. The stress of this experience is all the more difficult because people may not be aware manipulation is happening – neither the victim nor the perpetrator.

Some perpetrators are not aware they are using these tricks and can be quite confused when other people become so angry with them as they feel they are simply trying to get a message across. After a recent seminar, a client said to me with great awareness 'Now, after thirty years, I at last realise why people cannot stand when I win an argument' ... Another man rang after a lunchtime seminar to tell me 'I now realise what I have been doing to my girlfriend all these years'. (He didn't say he was going to stop!)

For the victim, of course, the stress of falling for these tricks is most frustrating, for example when someone is abusive towards you, or stereotypes you or accuses you of causing problems. Instead of dealing with this at the time, you find your mind in a muddle and you can only think clearly much later ... Awareness for both parties, the victim and perpetrator, is knowing how to spot the difference between clear and false reasoning *at the time.* This awareness reduces the stress in these situations for both sides, allowing everyone to move forward to a happy outcome.

REASONING IS A GAME

You may ask why, for most people, thinking on our feet is so difficult. I think reasoning is often simply a game, and the one who is cleverest at logic can be the winner. Logic is very persuasive and we are often seduced, confused or bewildered by other people's ability to take control of a situation, even when they might not be right. Many people feel this way when they describe to me their frustrations at meetings or serious discussions. Perhaps the same thing happens to you.

Clare described it to me this way:

I was so clear about what I wanted when I went into the meeting. I had thought it all through, with all my facts and figures in place. Then, during the course of conversation, I found I was becoming less sure of myself, and I began to feel anxious, and I'm ashamed to say I could feel myself becoming emotional and angry.

It was only a few days later that I realised what I should have said. Only then did I realise how I was being manipulated during the argument. But of course then it was too late.

Or listen to Jack's story:

Picture this. You are in the middle of a presentation on the subject of why the company should develop an executive range of men's shirts and market it aggressively in Europe. The chief executive interrupts 'I think it's best to stick with our current design. We tried something like this years ago and it did not work. Besides, where can we get the extra cash to fund your idea?'

What would *you* say? How would you feel if you were Jack? Would your knees buckle? Would your stomach feel as if it's digesting a triple pickle sandwich like his did? Or would you see in the very short response from this CEO, one very simple trick of manipulation (even if the CEO didn't see it himself). You could immediately deal with it, and then carry on effectively to discuss marketing your new range of men's shirts? (If not, don't worry, you will learn more about this trick later.)

I hope these accounts show you one of the most crucial needs for success in business and everyday life – the need for clear and effective thinking, especially when thinking on your feet!

What this book can do for you

This book assumes that you have a purpose and goals you want to achieve in life. However, what sometimes hinders you from getting what you want is that awful experience of losing the vitality and meaning you bring to the situation in order to make it happen.

Let's face it, like Jack and Clare, you've all had the experience of knowing *precisely* what you want when you go into a meeting with others. But sometimes instead of persuading them to believe in your brilliant idea, you lose the train of thought in the discussion and their criticisms of the idea sound as if they are making more sense than you are. That is ... until that night, when you realise exactly what you should have said to counteract their argument ... So it's not that you had a bad idea, it's just that you did not think quickly enough to bring your project to reality when it matters.

Being clear about the goal you want to achieve is only the first step in getting what you want. What copper fastens your achievement is the clear thinking you bring to attaining this goal. The meaning you bestow on your goal can become the difference between success and failure.

Let me explain this for a moment. Because a lot of people are not clear about the difference between purpose and meaning, many believe that since they have a purpose, they can easily attain their goals. 'I know what I want,' they say, 'I have a clear vision'. But it is the meaning you give to this purpose – and also the meaning you allow others to give to your goals – that will determine whether you can achieve what you desire.

For example, my purpose is to write this book, that is very clear, but my ability to carry out my purpose is bound up in the meaning I give to my purpose:

It is a difficult / worthless / easy / worthwhile task.

Each of these thoughts will either help or hinder my ability to carry out my purpose. *Your purpose may be to change your career, secure a promotion, overcome a phobia, realise a dream, control your wayward teenager … Whatever your purpose, the meaning you bring to it, how you think about it will determine your success. And how you get **others** to think about it will be the key to convincing them to come with you.*

Another distinction we will work on in this book is awareness of the difference between *passion* and *emotion*. The amount of passion and not emotion you are willing to put into your project will determine its success. You will learn not to get bogged down by emotion, but rather, how to get fired up by passion.

MY AIM IN WRITING THIS BOOK

The aim of this book is, first of all, to help you clarify your own thinking before you try to convince others. We will then tackle the ten tricks of manipulation that often happen when you try to persuade others of just how brilliant you really are!

The third section of this book is in the shape of a workshop booklet where you can record and practice your new skills. There is space for you to clarify your thoughts before you go into a meeting or have an important discussion. There is also room for you to note down instances of manipulation when you encounter them and most important of all, there is space for you to write your own success stories, one by one, as you build up your confidence in handling these situations.

To build on your skills successfully we will concentrate on three aims in particular. How to:

CLEAR THE CLUTTER
    IDENTIFY purpose
    CLARIFY meaning
    THINK with passion not emotion
    CHANGE negative thinking into positive action

WEED OUT THE WAFFLE
    Spot the ten tricks of manipulation when 'thinking on your feet'.

GET GOING ON RESULTS
    Think Quickly on your Feet Workshop
    Write your own success stories

PART I

CLEAR THE CLUTTER

Identify, Clarify, Think and Change

The 'quick thinking' dog

Let me tell you the story about the quick thinking dog. Once upon a time a wealthy man decided to go on an adventurous safari. He took his favourite pet dog along for company. One day the dog starts chasing butterflies and before long he discovers that he is lost. So, wandering about he notices a leopard heading rapidly in his direction with the obvious intention of having lunch.

The dog thinks, 'Oh Christ, I'm in deep trouble now.' (He was an Irish Setter) …. Then he notices some bones on the ground close by and immediately settles down to chew on the bones with his back to the approaching cat.

Just as the leopard is about to leap, the dog exclaims loudly, 'Jesus, that was one delicious leopard. I wonder if there are any more around here?'

Hearing this the leopard halts his attack in mid stride, as a look of terror comes over him, and slinks away into the trees.

'Whew,' says the leopard, 'That was close. That dog nearly had me'.

Meanwhile, a monkey who had been watching the whole scene from a nearby tree, realises he can put this knowledge to good use and trade it for protection from the leopard. So, off he goes. But the dog saw him heading after the leopard with great speed, and figured that something must be up (Irish paranoia).

The monkey soon catches up with the leopard, spills the beans and strikes a deal for himself with the leopard. 'Here monkey, hop on my back and see what's going to happen to that conniving canine.'

Now the dog sees the leopard coming with the monkey on his back and thinks 'What the hell am I going to do now?' But instead of running, the dog sits down with his back to his attackers pretending he hasn't seen them yet. And just when they get close enough to hear, the dog says, 'Where's that damn monkey. I just can't trust him. I sent him off half and hour ago to bring me another leopard, and he's still not back!

What a wonderful story. And what a brilliant way to think. This canine certainly knows his purpose. He is under no illusion as to what he is trying to achieve – *his survival is paramount.* This blinding clarity helps him to think very quickly and cunningly in order to reach that goal. He is not dithering around thinking 'what am I doing here?' or 'how did I get here?' or, to coin a current business trend 'what are my options?' There is one, and only one overriding thought – 'get out of here, in one piece'.

Quick thinking is needed for survival – your survival. In fact, you might often feel like this unfortunate dog when you go into certain meetings at work, or have exhausting discussions with highly charged loved ones determined to secure what they want. When you are clear about your purpose and goals in life, it makes it so much easier to think wisely and to your advantage.

But to be clear about your purpose is only the start. The dog in the story is very clear about his purpose – it is his survival. Like the dog, it is the way you *understand and give meaning* to your goal that will determine your success in achieving that purpose. Our clever dog does not wonder about his immediate environment and whether he will survive it. He doesn't guess whether others will help him or hinder him. Our cheeky dog could have understood several things about his situation: 'the leopard is stronger than me', 'both the monkey and the leopard will beat me', 'this situation is weighted too much against me', 'I'm lost' – but if he had continued to read his situation in any of these ways he would not have survived. What made him achieve his purpose was his switch to the strong, positive meaning he gave to his situation – and in doing so he was able to outwit the others.

FOUR SIMPLE STRATEGIES – USE ICTC

Part I of this book takes you through this kind of thinking. The kind of thinking you need to be confident, sure and dedicated to achieve what you want. This is the frame of mind you need to be in before you begin to think on your feet so that no matter what is said in your discussions you can remain focused and achieve your goal. 'Clear the Clutter' defines four simple strategies you can use to give you this confidence. These are: Identify, Clarify, Think and Change – **ICTC** – four logical steps to becoming clear and focused.

> IDENTIFY your purpose
>
> CLARIFY its meaning
>
> THINK with passion not emotion
>
> CHANGE negative thinking into positive action

With these you will **KNOW**

> ❖ What you want
>
> ❖ What it entails
>
> ❖ How you feel about it
>
> ❖ Use your wit and intelligence to go and get it

⚿ IDENTIFY YOUR PURPOSE

The key to successful 'quick thinking on your feet' is in knowing your purpose. Before you begin to discuss your goals, projects or aspirations with others you must have a clear idea of what they really are. If you don't, you will lack the confidence to argue clearly and to the point. This may sound like common sense to you, but it is amazing the number of times we only have a vague idea about what we want. Yes, you might think it would be lovely to have a holiday in the Seychelles, get a promotion next year, find a partner, make a lot of money. These are wonderful dreams, but to make them into a purpose you need to have concrete ideas on how you are going to achieve these fantasies.

DISTINGUISH IDEALS FROM IDEAS

What we sometimes do when thinking about our goals is to confuse an ideal with an idea. Concepts like happiness, wealth and freedom from stress are *ideals*, not *ideas*. An ideal is something we strive for, an idea is something we can put into action. We can all understand what ideals mean, but it is extremely hard, if not impossible, to define them because they may differ from person to person. My meaning of 'freedom from stress', for example parachuting, could be totally stress *inducing* for you. So, in defining your purpose you need to be sure you have a good idea and not a great ideal. You need a good idea that you can clearly define, and not just vaguely understand. Otherwise you may cause great confusion all around.

For example, if you want 'to be happy' you must think of an idea that you know will give you happiness. Striving for happiness will not bring happiness. You must consider actions you can take to achieve happiness. You may consider a change of career (stimulation), a move to a different city (adventure), helping others (feeling of well being) ... the list is endless.

If you want that promotion, don't think of it as an ideal you aspire to, make it an idea you can work on. Then make that your purpose and set the objectives you need to achieve to reach that goal. In the same way, if you want to start your own business, make that into a concrete idea you can work on. Gain clarity around how you are going to develop your idea into action, defining what you want to do and your ability to succeed.

One simple technique to achieve clarity around your purpose is to use the training tool of asking 'why?' five times.* This is an excellent method to help clarify purpose and understanding (we also revisit it as an antidote to one of the tricks of manipulation later on). If you can answer 'why' five times to why you want to achieve your goal, your thinking will be much clearer and sharper when communicating that goal to others. For example, let's say you want to be successful at painting pictures. The conversation we might have is:

I'd like to be able to paint.
Why?
Because I feel confident and relaxed when I paint, others admire my work.
Why are you so confident and relaxed about this?
Because I feel chuffed, I actually painted the picture myself.

* This technique was originally developed in the 1970s by Maswaki Imai of Toyota.

Why does painting the picture make you so confident and re-
    laxed?
Because I feel I achieved something.
Why does this achievement make you feel confident and relaxed?
Because it makes me feel good about myself.

The real purpose here then is to be able to paint. 'I will enjoy painting as I feel confident and relaxed that I can achieve good results. I know I can achieve good results as my family and friends have admired previous pictures of mine. A sense of achievement is important to me and I know I can get this through my painting. At the end of the day I want to feel good about myself and painting is a way of achieving this'.

If you explain your purpose to me in this way, I would be happy that you have a clear idea of what you want to do (paint), why (to feel good about yourself) and what expectations you can hope to achieve (good results that can be admired by yourself and others). This clarity identifies your purpose. You are ready to go and will have no problem convincing other people either!

SUMMARY

☺ Be aware of the difference between 'ideals' and 'ideas': ideals you aspire to; ideas you act on

☺ Be clear about your purpose: ask 'why?' five times

⚷— CLARIFY MEANING

Once you know your purpose you need to be clear on the meaning you are giving to this purpose. I believe that the meaning you give to any idea can and will determine its success or failure. Quite a strong statement you might think but unfortunately it is all too true. I have known many people with great ideas, but only a few succeed. Why is that? They all know they want to achieve something, they all have a purpose, but only some of them are able to reach their goals. It can't be that some have not been able to identify their purpose, because as I say, they all begin with a vision, yet some materialise that vision and others don't. So, what is going on?

THE DIFFERENCE BETWEEN SUCCESS AND FAILURE

I believe the difficulty and the difference between success and failure can come down to the meaning we give to our goals and visions. First of all, I must explain that there is a difference between purpose and meaning. A lot of the time we confuse the two, for example, 'the purpose of life' and 'the meaning of life' are sometimes spoken of as if they are identical. To show you what I mean, I will refer to the difference between these two phenomena as explained beautifully by Lou Marinoff in his book *Plato not Prozac*. I will paraphrase his description here and if you want to read further please refer to his excellent book.

Marinoff gives the analogy of a menu. He says the purpose

of a menu is to help you choose something to eat. The meaning of the menu is to give you information about that choice. If you go into a restaurant with a group of people and are given a menu in Chinese (and no one speaks the language), then you may all well know the purpose of the menu – to help you make a choice – but as no one understands what it means, making that choice is impossible. This makes the purpose of choosing food incredibly difficult and you may well end up in a situation where you will change restaurant. You cannot achieve your goal, not because you do not understand the purpose of why you are there, but because the information to make sense of your purpose is incomprehensible.

DON'T CONFUSE YOUR BRAIN

Likewise, if you have a clear goal or purpose – to be able to drive – you still may not be able to achieve this goal if you insist on giving it conflicting signals, that in some way *go against* reaching your aims. As in the analogy above, you may well find that you have to abandon your goal because the information your brain is receiving to make sense of your purpose is incomprehensible.

To continue with the example of wanting to be able to drive – if that is your purpose but the meaning you bring to the situation is 'I don't have the time', 'there's no safe place to learn to drive', 'I'll be no good anyway' then it is very unlikely that you will *ever* be able to drive as the information your brain is receiving is actually incompatible with the goal you are trying to achieve. In fact, your understanding of the situation is contradicting the very goal you are trying to reach. No wonder we get confused!

In order to clear the clutter in your head and be clear about what you want, you need to be able to synchronise your purpose with a compatible meaning. A meaning that will make sense of the goal you are trying to achieve. The 'quick thinking dog' had a choice of several meanings he could put on his situation and he chose the meaning that *enhanced* his survival. He chose the meaning that would *secure* his goal not *destroy* it.

This is sometimes not an easy thing to do, but if you can achieve a meaning that will enhance your purpose, you will gain huge confidence.

BELIEVE IN YOURSELF

So, what do you have to do? We need to visit the area of your thinking that informs your perceptions and beliefs. Because how you *perceive* your purpose will be the key to whether you can achieve it or not. In fact, in this twenty-first century we are all so scientific we insist on using this word 'perception' to talk about how we understand the world. However, a word we no longer use, which I think is more applicable to how we give meaning to ourselves, our aims and ambitions, is the word 'myth'. Of course, we tend to think this is too old fashioned or too 'unscientific' a concept. We talk about Greek mythology or Celtic mythology as if mythology is a thing of the past. I believe 'myth' is an apt description of the way we see ourselves today. In my training seminars, I tell delegates that everyone in the room (including myself) is what I call a 'myth carrier'. We all have myths or 'notions' about ourselves, that may or may not be true, but either way they are incredibly powerful in determining our ability to succeed or fail. Why? Because the truth of these myths is almost irrelevant, their power lies in how deeply and seriously you believe in them.

I talk of 'myth' as the ability to believe in something *as if* it is true. A negative myth would be something like 'there is no use going for that job, because I would never get it anyway'. Now if you truly believe this you won't go for the job, with the result that you will never know if what you were thinking was in fact true, because you never tried.

The real tragedy of negative myths is that although they are never tested or tried out in reality, you will still go on believing them (sometimes for the rest of your life) *as if* they are true. That is why they will tend to lead you to victimisation or inaction. You will feel like you cannot do something and therefore not try to, believing it is not possible. Negative myths are incompatible with your purpose because the information they are giving your brain is actually contrary to the goal you are trying to reach. If you want that job, but won't apply because you think you will never get it you are not making sense towards reaching your goal. In fact, you are confusing your brain with conflicting messages. On the one hand, you are thinking you want the goal, on the other you are convincing yourself that you can never get it.

I know there are many reasons why we give ourselves these conflicting messages, fear, risk aversion, a lack of confidence or a lack of self-esteem But let's try and admit these into the equation, and at the same time develop a meaning that is compatible with your goal and not contrary to it. We can admit we are afraid and *still* strive for that goal.

MAKE YOUR THINKING COMPATIBLE, NOT CONTRADICTORY TO YOUR PURPOSE

To clear out the clutter, do not confuse your brain with these conflicting messages. When you have a purpose choose a meaning that makes sense of that purpose. You will find that this way of thinking will give you more confidence to get what you want.

In our example of wanting the job, a compatible meaning to give to achieve your purpose might be, 'I want to apply for this job because it is something that interests me and I believe I have the qualifications required. I am a bit worried about going for it though as there are other very strong candidates and I am afraid I might not succeed. However, if I do succeed it will be a terrific boost to my confidence and I will secure a position I have always wanted. And even if I am not successful this time, I will have had great experience and the company will see I am interested in being promoted/moving and may offer me something more interesting. Either way I will have gained something'.

When you have a purpose try to give it meaning that will enhance your goal, not hinder it. Easier said than done I hear you say. And you are right. However, if we are able to have a positive attitude it certainly helps to clear our thinking and reduce the fear and risk involved in thinking our ideas through to action. But some of us still find this impossible without mastering further strategies. Identifying your purpose and clarifying its meaning in a way that enables you to move forward is very confidence building. Let's look at two more strategies that can help you move nearer your goal.

SUMMARY

☺ Know the difference between your purpose and the meaning you give to it

☺ Believe in your abilities to succeed

☺ Don't confuse your brain

☺ Use meaning that is compatible, not contradictory to your purpose

THINK WITH PASSION NOT EMOTION

Once you have identified your purpose and clarified the meaning you need to give to it, there is still something that needs to be addressed. It concerns how you *feel* about what you want to achieve. Because we are not robots, it is sometimes very difficult to stop our feelings getting in the way of what we want to get done.

You know what it is like. Your purpose is to get fit. This is an admirable purpose. You understand what it means to get fit, you know you need to go to the gym twice a week, do lots of exercise and take care of your diet. You know you are well capable of doing this so there should be no problem – right? The only thing is you hate the whole idea of getting fit. You just couldn't be bothered.

Because of this, your thought processes slow down and you can no longer think of ways to make getting fit more interesting because you are not committed. However, imagine if you were really excited about getting fit, you would be thinking of loads of wonderful creative ways in which you could really enjoy yourself. Your mind would be buzzing with all the different games you could play and you might even create some innovative new ways of keeping fit yourself.

What I am saying is that the way you feel about something has an effect on how clearly and creatively you can think about it. Let me explain this by telling you something I learned from one of my students.

PASSION: FEELINGS ATTACHED TO YOUR PROJECT

I gave a course in Sheffield, England in 1994 and I covered this very topic with the group, about how we can stop our feelings from getting in the way of what we are trying to achieve through clear thinking. We discussed whether we should perhaps get rid of feelings altogether and came to the conclusion quite quickly that this was not a possibility. 'How could we get up in the morning,' someone said, 'unless we had a desire to do so', if we had no desires or passions the world would be horribly bleak and not worth living. 'Yet on the other hand,' another replied 'if I'm faced with someone who is emotional, or becoming emotional in a discussion, we can simply lose the plot. I have to spend my time trying to placate their emotions rather than discussing the issue we are there to resolve. And nothing gets done'.

So what do we do? Leave out feelings or leave them in? Just then a member of the group, Salima, gave us this wonderful distinction that I hope will help you to clarify your feelings also when tackling a problem, issue or situation. For me it is a jewel of wisdom and I have used it in all my training courses ever since.

What she said is this:

When I am carrying out a project, either at work or at home, I try to distinguish between whether I am passionate about my project or emotional about my project. If I am passionate about what I am doing my feelings are attached to the project. If someone criticises me and I am passionate, I listen because I think and believe this is a terrific project but they don't – so they must be seeing something I am missing. If I can find out what this is and overcome their problem then my project will be stronger and I will have a greater chance of success. If I have insurmountable problems and I am passionate about what I am doing, it is amazing the number of ideas I can come up with to get what I want. My focus is entirely on the goal I am trying to reach.

In fact, you may notice that the more passionate people are the more they believe they have already succeeded. You know when you believe, really believe in something, failure is not an option. You are not thinking *'will* I get there?' You concentrate on *how* and *when* you will succeed, not *if.* This is what passion and enthusiasm do for your projects, they fire up your thinking to achieve your goal.

EMOTIONS: FEELINGS ATTACHED TO YOUR EGO

Salima continued:

however when I am emotional about my project, instead of my feelings being attached to my project, they are attached to my ego – my identity with the project. So let's say the same thing happens as above, I am in the middle of my project and someone criticises what I'm doing. Now, instead of listening, I become defensive, I start to think – they don't want me to do this, maybe they want it for themselves. Maybe they think I am not capable of doing this. In other words, my thinking is now completely different from the scenario above when my focus was on achieving the goal. My focus is now on saving my ego and my thinking will be entirely different and unfortunately go in the opposite direction to what I am trying to achieve.

When you are passionate your focus is external, on the goal you are trying to achieve. When you are emotional your focus is internal, your sights are on saving your ego.

I believe this is a marvellous distinction to be aware of. If you find your thinking is becoming confused or cluttered with irrelevant issues, ask yourself are you 'passionate' or 'emotional' about what you want to achieve. Ask yourself, 'is my focus on myself or on the goal I am trying to reach?' The answer to this question should give you clarity. How you answer will make you aware of whether your interest lies in getting the job done, or in what other people think of you and your ability to get the job done. If you are more interested in what other people think, your emotions for your ego are stronger than your passion for your project.

Perhaps a story to illustrate this point will help. A friend of mine described how when she was setting out in her business over ten years ago, she spent a lot of time on the phone trying to convince people to buy her product. Invariably, with a new product she was able to translate only a minority of these calls into meetings. But once she got the meeting with a prospective client, she was able to gain their interest in her product and get them to buy. This is what it is like for most people starting off in business.

My friend concentrated her efforts in making each meeting she secured turn into to a profitable sale. She had to go through a lot of rejection calls to get one productive meeting. She understood this very clearly. However, she was astonished one day, when an acquaintance said to her with the utmost sympathy 'I just don't know how you can take the rejection'.

My friend was amazed:

> What rejection? No one is rejecting me, they don't even know who I am, so how can they be rejecting me. They are saying no to my product. So what I do is listen, find out why my product

doesn't suit them, and then work on redesigning what I have to offer in order to meet their needs. Their rejection of my product is actually a way of helping me to become more successful, as I can learn so much and become a lot more creative in what I do.

That is passion and not emotion. By not taking rejection personally, this woman was able to connect the rejection she experienced to her project and not her ego. She is now running a very successful business throughout Europe. If you find you are concentrating on yourself in any situation, remember refocus, separate ego from issue, and refocus on the goal you are trying to achieve and how you are going to get there. Don't think 'will I be able to get there?' Think '*how* do I get there?'

SUMMARY

REMEMBER TO HAVE PASSION FOR YOUR PROJECT

☺ When you are passionate your feelings are attached to your project – you overcome problems to reach your goal

NOT EMOTIONS FOR YOUR EGO

☺ When you are emotional your feelings are attached to your ego – you may become overwhelmed by problems and so not reach your goal

8 CHANGE NEGATIVE
THINKING INTO POSITIVE ACTION

> *You cannot prevent the birds of sadness from flying over your head,*
> *but you can prevent them from nesting in your hair*
>
> CHINESE PROVERB

The fourth and last strategy to help us get that clear thinking and confidence to achieve our goals is probably the most powerful one of all. This is the ability to change negative thinking into positive action. As we discussed in the chapter on 'meaning' it is sometimes very difficult to overcome negative 'myths' about ourselves and what we can achieve. Sometimes negative beliefs about what we can and can not do are so ingrained that they become real blocks to our progress. We may try to think with passion and not emotion, but sometimes this may be very difficult.

People often talk about the 'yes-but' factor being part of their everyday lives. Do you know the 'yes-but' factor? It is what happens when you have a great idea, but ... 'Yes that's a great idea, *but* I just don't have the time', or 'Yes, that's a brilliant suggestion, *but* we simply don't have the money ...' And so on. Negative thinking comes in and blocks a route forward, so nothing can be achieved.

One of the most famous business examples of the 'yes-but' factor relates to two well-known organisations who, before the Xerox Corporation, were offered the prototype of the photocopying machine. They refused to take it. Why? Their answer was 'Yes, we think this is a good idea, but we can see no commercial application for it …' Aren't they sorry now? The risk was too great, they were afraid of losing money. Of course, when Rank Xerox had the passion to see the project through and overcome the negatives in developing commercial application, they were able to produce a worldwide winning product.

Several companies ask me to talk to their people just on this matter alone. The top teams tell me again and again, 'we have terrific people here, we know they can achieve great things, but we need to harness their negative thinking into positive action'.

The Metropolitan Police in London have an example of turning negative thinking into positive action. In the late 1990s they had a soaring rate of burglaries and were finding it very difficult to bring the figures down. They were very negative and thought nothing could be done. Why not? Because they couldn't catch the burglars, no matter what they tried to do. Why couldn't they catch them, because the burglars kept running away from them … If you listen to this negative statement 'the burglars keep running away from us' as a vital piece of information on how to catch the burglars, instead of hearing it as an emotional situation that you cannot solve, you will get your answer.

This negative was valuable information because what it really said was that if they could get the burglars to run towards them, they could solve the problem. *We can't catch the burglars because they run from us = we can catch them if the run towards us.* And that is what they did. They set up several dummy 'pawn shops' where burglars came to sell stolen goods – so the burg-

34

lars ran straight towards the police and they caught them, reducing the incidence of burglary enormously.

So, if you are finding it difficult to switch from emotion to passion for your project, this other technique of making your negative or fearful thinking work for you and not against you can be powerful. Instead of being overwhelmed by negative information, use it as the vital piece of knowledge you need to find a solution. How many times when you are negative do you say 'I'm just being realistic. We can't do it.' I believe you can listen to this realism but instead of it blocking your way forward you can use the negative factor to actually solve your problem.

In this chapter, I want to show you how to do just that. I want to show you that far from being a block to your progression negative thinking can be the vital information you need to get things done.

What I am going to explain to you is a training tool call the DNA print. This is a technique I devised based on something negative that happened to me years ago. I was able to get through this negative experience and also had a huge gain in being able to develop this training tool – one which I have used ever since on all my training courses. People have found it most effective for honing in on their negative thinking and using it as valuable knowledge to achieve their goals.

USING THE DNA PRINT

Have you ever had the experience of arriving at a foreign airport minus your baggage? I certainly did. Some years ago I was standing at the desk at Gatwick airport, trying to locate my bag.

In the bag were my notes for the most crucial conference I had ever given to a huge multinational audience. My clothes were in that bag – including my precious black-and-white suit. This was a most formal conference, and here was I, standing in a pair of shorts – all I had.

Yet, let me tell you how this negative experience has given me one of the most effective tools in making my own business so successful.

The woman at the airport desk was utterly sympathetic. She talked of other options – getting other clothes, having the notes e-mailed, and so on. Although sympathetic, I noticed her thinking was entirely negative: all the time she assumed we could never get the bag.

Why not? One, she said, the offices in Dublin were closed (it was after 6 p.m.). Two, there was no carrier (the last flight had gone). Three, the airline had a 'no-same-day' policy (i.e., even if the bag had arrived by then, I couldn't get it on the same day).

I was beginning to panic. Then I thought – Valerie, listen to her. She's actually telling you how to get the bag. Just listen! What you're really hearing is – you can get your bag, one, if we find an office that's open; two, if we get a carrier; and three, if we get rid of this no-same-day policy!

So I asked her – do you have a list of all your Dublin offices? She gave me the list and when we began telephoning, we found one office still open … That office sourced the bag, and they put it on another airline into Gatwick that evening.

By then, the woman realised her no-same-day policy made no sense, and I had the bag at my hotel by 9 p.m.

What had actually happened? Simple – the woman's three

no-nos had actually directed me to a solution. Negative think-ing is often the signpost in this way. So, instead of being *over-whelmed* by negative thinking, we should use it as a focus to *overcoming* the problem.

The following year, in Dublin, I was addressing an audience of dynamic businesswomen, the most talented and vibrant of whom was undoubtedly Jane.

I told the delegates what had happened at Gatwick, and about the process of my thinking, which led to the fast recovery of my bag. This process I now label 'DNA' thinking – *Dream/Negatives/Actions*.

For example, if there is something you want (that's the *Dream* – in my case the bag), but you cannot get it because of *Negative* thinking (the Gatwick woman's no-nos), then focus on those very reasons why not, and by overcoming them, you create the *Actions* to solve the problem yourself (in my case, getting that bag).

At the end of my story, the delegates did 'DNA' exercises relating to their own particular needs.

Some weeks later I got a letter from Jane. She told me she had been about to give up her career – she felt she had lost her business acumen, drive, talent, everything. But after she heard my Gatwick story, and had done some exercises based on her own experiences, she saw how to change her negative thinking into positive action.

What did she do? The following Monday she revisited her business plan, introduced long-pondered new products, saw her bank manager and made a totally new start ... And it's still working.

The value of negative thinking is that it has a great knowledge base. In fact, as I already said, when people are negative they will often say to you 'look, I'm just being realistic'. And they are – that's what you must pay attention to. When someone is pointing out the negatives as to why you can't achieve what you want, they are actually showing you how to get it. Listen to them to find out what the problem is. Once you know what the problem is you can concentrate on fixing it and getting what you want.

For example, Susan, a course delegate, told me how she had used the DNA technique shortly after a training session. She had tried to return goods to a shop and the shop assistant very firmly said no. Susan asked why not. The assistant's main reason was that the manager had to give permission and the manager was not in the shop that day. Instead of reacting emotionally to this, Susan heard it as the vital piece of information she needed to solve her problem. If she wasn't getting what she wanted because the manager wasn't there, then the manager was the key to being able to successfully get what she wanted. Where was the manager? At head office Susan was told, so she promptly rang head office, spoke to the manager and got her permission. The assistant was obliged to change the goods.

It is simple, instead of being an emotional block to what you want, the negative in the situation (why you *cannot* do something) is often the vital knowledge you need to get the job done. If you can listen to negative input in a discussion in an objective way you will find the information you need to progress your goals.

That is what 'changing negative thinking into positive action' is all about. If you have the intelligence to see where the problems are, remember you must also have the intelligence to fix them. So many of us find it difficult to *see* the real problems in the first place. If you see them you are 50 per cent on the way to fixing them. Make sure that 'negative thinking' becomes your signpost to achieve your goals, not the brick wall that stops you. When you think you cannot achieve something, ask yourself why not? What you will find is the answer that may help you achieve that goal. Think of my Gatwick experience. In listing the negatives, we found what we needed to do to get the bag. When you list your negatives, you will find your own personal blocks to achieving your dreams. Just listing these blocks gives you greater insight into the problems you may be having in trying to achieve your goal. But remember, with this list in front of you, you are now looking at all the information you need to find a solution. If you can work creatively through these negative blocks you are well on your way to succeeding at what you want. Good Luck!

SUMMARY

☺ Use the DNA print successfully, go from D (dream), through N (negatives), to get to A (actions)

This first part of the book has addressed the thinking tools to help you clarify your own thinking before you get into discussion with others. It is important to be confident in what you believe. You are less likely to be manipulated if you portray confidence and can justify your ideas and back them up with clear thought and argument.

I hope that by following the rules of **ICTC** –

- ❖ **Identify** your purpose (know what you want)
- ❖ **Clarify** its meaning (what it entails)
- ❖ **Think** with passion not emotion (how you feel)
- ❖ **Change** negative thinking into positive action (use your wits to get it)

you will develop a clear belief in what you want, as well as the determined confidence to go and get it.

The workshop in Part III of this book allows you to test your ideas, and develop them in order to become confident and ready to communicate them with a clear mind and focused delivery.

PART II

WEED OUT THE WAFFLE

QUICK
THINKING

Summary of
THE TEN TRICKS

- ❖ Someone attempts to exert a false authority over you
- ❖ You may feel fearful, uncertain or doubtful (FUD)
- ❖ Someone is abusive towards you
- ❖ They stereotype you
- ❖ They win an argument, not by proving they are right, but by emphasising how wrong you are
- ❖ You are accused of having caused problems
- ❖ The argument sounds great, but you're not sure if the words have any real meaning.
- ❖ You feel forced into making a choice between two extremes
- ❖ You are seduced by a great story or brilliant example
- ❖ You are faced with the repetition of a point, but don't hear any justification for it

THE TEN TRICKS OF MANIPULATION

INTRODUCTION

This section covers the most important aspect of 'quick thinking on your feet' – the part where you learn to overcome your brilliance at 'staircase wit'.

Now that you know how to gain clarity in your own thinking, I will introduce you to the ten tricks of manipulation, so that no matter how often these tricks are used, you can keep a clear head and reach your goal undeterred. The main point to remember about these tricks is that they are all completely irrational and illogical. Unfortunately, they may sound as if they are making sense – but, remember that is their power. Once you see them for what they are they lose that power and you can regain full control of the discussion.

REFERENCE

I have tried to create a structure to this part of the book that will help you to use it as a reference tool. Each chapter is devoted to one trick of manipulation only, so that you can flick in and out of these chapters in any sequence you want. You won't need to read the whole book in any order, but only as you require it for a particular meeting, discussion or important conversation. I find myself that I can handle some of these manipulation tricks better than others, so that I only need to revisit a few and do not need to look at others at all. You may feel the same.

LEARNING TOOL

I hope that this book will be an important learning tool *after* a meeting also. For example, when leaving a meeting, if you feel uneasy about some of the thinking that went on during discussions, but can't specifically put your finger on what went wrong, then reading through these chapters should be able to help you pinpoint what happened and so give you more confidence to recognise and tackle the same thinking next time it occurs

STRUCTURE

For clarity, each of the following ten chapters is divided into four sub headings.

Each trick of manipulation is described in the following way, using the acronym WHAT:

W – What it is
H – How it happens
A – Actions you take
T – True success story

I am using the acronym WHAT as a memory aid for you, as when you are thinking on your feet, it is helpful to have a reference you can remember quickly. 'What!?' is also what you may feel like shouting with indignation when these tricks occur, so I think this acronym should help to keep you on a calm and fruitful path.

Not all chapters are the same length, as some tricks are more complex than others. Some can be explained and dealt with quite easily, while others require a lot more detail.

I introduce most chapters with a joke that illustrates the particular trick we discuss. So as well as learning something new, you may also have a little chuckle along the way.

Happy Reading!

1

THE AUTHORITY CARD

> *I think there is a world market for maybe five computers*
> THOMAS WATSON, CHAIRMAN OF IBM, 1943

How embarrassing! Can you imagine the number of people who would have believed Mr Watson – after all he was chairman of IBM, the leading computer company in the world at the time. And if anyone had disagreed with this statement, they would surely have been shot down as not having the same authority as the speaker. But as we all know now (with the benefit of hindsight, of course) this statement is in fact not true. No amount of authority can make a belief true, it only makes it believable. The power of the 'authority card' trick is to make you think that something that sounds plausible (believable) is in fact true. However, it is only when a belief is backed up by real evidence that it has some chance of being true. In the example above it is not.

WHAT IT IS

Playing the 'authority card' is quite an effective trick when 'thinking on your feet'. When people reason with 'false authority' they don't give real evidence for their beliefs. The power of this trick depends on tapping into the psychological difficulty of an individual to fight against the group, or against a way of doing things.

The fact that a false authority has no evidence is both its strength and its weakness. It is strong and because it is impossible to argue against, it makes you feel powerless. How can you change or attack a great name or great tradition? It is weak, because when you look behind it for proof or evidence, there is none – all you find is innuendo and assumption.

An example of true authority is when a qualified expert makes a decision based on qualified expertise, knowledge and experience. Current examples would be, an engineering project using the authority and reasoning of an engineering expert, or a medical authority giving medical expertise that is backed up by sound evidence and expert thinking. In both cases, the people are qualified and what they say can be tested. Their authority can be validated or rejected based on clear evidence. However, when using false authority a speaker will not have any evidence that can be tested to be accepted or rejected. Their power of authority depends on two classic techniques of false argument: **tradition** and **power of the group**. These techniques confuse their audience into believing what they want them to think with no evidence whatsoever.

𝓗OW IT HAPPENS

1: Tradition

Tradition is a technique very frequently used in times of change. Does the phrase 'We've always done it this way' mean anything to you? I thought so. There seems to be unanimous agreement in every business, home or organisation that this phrase is the most used response when people are afraid of change.

Just imagine you have developed a great new way of doing your work. You want to convince your colleagues who don't want to know. They say 'there is no need to change', 'why not?' 'because we've always done it this way ...' This immediate response is so easy. The implication is that 'because we've always done it this way' this is the right way. But is it? Where is the proof for this. Just because I say 'the wall has always been white' doesn't mean that it is right to be white! I am only stating a fact, not a reason. Good arguments need good reasoning and sound evidence, not just a statement of the obvious.

What is really going on here is that people using this phrase are not using any logic at all. They are triggering your emotions. They want to intimidate you into believing that you cannot stand up to such a great force.

If you fall for tradition, you will either become intimidated or aggressive. 'We've always done it this way' implies 'who are you to stand up to the whole strong lobby of tradition?' You may feel 'I'm not strong enough to deal with this' or alternatively, 'It's about bloody time I dealt with this'.

If you have any of these reactions you have become a victim of this trick, because now you are reacting emotionally and your success will depend on the strength of your personality rather than the viability of the ideas you are trying to introduce.

Tradition is worse if it is further backed up by the power of the group. Here the emphasis is on the *we* in 'we have always done it this way'. This can become quite a horrible experience as the tricksters will do their very best to make you feel alienated from the rest of the group. To avoid this alienation you may decide to give in and not go ahead with the intended change.

If it makes you feel any better this trick has been carried out on the best of us:

We don't like their sound, and guitar music is on the way out.

DECCA RECORDING CO. REJECTING THE BEATLES, 1962

Luckily the Beatles didn't let this powerful record company stop them from introducing change in musical tastes.

𝔄CTIONS YOU TAKE

☞ *Never defend yourself*

If you are the victim of this trick, the first thing to remember is never defend yourself against the other party. You may get caught up in an endless proving/disproving scenario. The mistake a lot of people make when faced with others who won't change is to give a list of benefits, showing how better things will be if they give it a chance.

This is the wrong thing to do at the very beginning of the discussion. If you give your opponent what you believe will be the benefits of the change you are giving them ammunition to attack you. For example, if I want someone to do their work in a different way and one of the benefits, I say, is that they will be able to do their work a lot faster. They may retort 'faster! You just come back here on Friday evening and see how long I will be here trying to figure this thing out' … It is now harder for me to show that this won't happen as they have hijacked one of my benefits and used it against me.

☞ Ask them 'wisdom' questions

The easiest way to overcome this trick of tradition is to make the person using it defend themselves. You don't have to prove anything to them. It is not enough for them to say 'we've always done it this way', they must show *why* they are doing it that way and give evidence for that way being the best way.

It is not enough to simply ask 'why?' however, as asking why often makes people feel very uneasy. They will often answer quite angrily 'I don't know why … it just works'.

'Why?' is an analysis question – and people often aren't able to analyse what they are doing and can become very uncomfortable when asked to do so. A much easier way to get information is to ask what I call 'a wisdom question'.

Wisdom questions are 'what?' questions. For example, 'What is it you like best about what you are doing?' or 'What makes you feel most comfortable, what do you enjoy most …?' These questions do give you an analysis of the situation, but to the listener they sound more like you are asking for their wisdom and valuable experience regarding their work, rather than their analysis of a situation. Other examples of 'wisdom questions' would be:

'What aspect of your job do you think is most important?'
'What do you think others appreciate most about your work?'
'What do you look for from others to help you in your work?'
These questions are much more flattering to your listener and will give you the vital information you need to move them forward with your ideas.

☞ *Acknowledge their understanding: use 'yes-and' not 'yes-but'*

If someone enjoys doing their work in a particular way, it is very important not to rubbish this by contradicting it.

Once you get the information you need you must then complement it not disagree with it. For example, if you tell me you like carrying out your work in a specific way because it is fast, and I reply by saying '*yes*, I understand that, *but* if you change to this new method it will be much faster …' it will sound like I'm dismissing the information you have just given me. The message is 'I know better …' And naturally you will again be ready to do battle with my new ideas.

A much more acceptable way to move an opponent forward is instead of using *yes-but* use '*yes-and*' with the very same information. As in the example above you could say '*Yes*, I see you appreciate being able to do things quickly *and* I believe we can build on that speed you have developed by adding …'

☞ *Now give the benefits of the change*

Once you understand the reasons behind someone's thinking, you can acknowledge it and add to it. Your benefits will then sound much more acceptable when you introduce them at this stage of the conversation. They can now become an *addition* to the other person's experience and not a contradiction that they will be fearful of.

2: Power of the group

Mob appeal is much more difficult to overcome than tradition. Even though it is based on the same false authority as tradition and is not backed up by evidence, its appeal is often a lot stronger. Its power lies in making you feel stupid, wrong or isolated if you do not agree with the rest of the group.

> *I have travelled the length and breadth of this country … and talked with the best people, and I can assure you that data processing is a fad that won't last out the year.*
>
> EDITOR IN CHARGE OF BUSINESS BOOKS FOR PRENTICE HALL, 1957

There is no evidence for what this editor is saying. The power of this quote is in the 'mob appeal'. His persuasion technique is that the best and the beautiful believe this, so therefore should you. (A lot of advertising uses this technique shamelessly every day.)

Because the power of the group has such a strong psychological effect, it can affect our clear thinking in an instant. If we disagree, we may start to question our own perception without having the wits to question the reasoning of the mob. In a work situation this can be very serious as important decisions can be made because of politics, fear, apathy or any number of things – rational thought not included.

HOW IT HAPPENS

It is at meetings that the power of the group often raises its destructive head. This can be work meetings, or even with friends

52

and in family discussions. The message is 'everyone here thinks this is right, except you, therefore you must be wrong'.

It is, of course, irrational to believe something to be right or wrong simply because the majority believe it to be so. It is not enough that everyone believes in something, they must have reason and evidence to show that it is true. Simply saying 'everyone thinks so' is irrelevant, although psychologically very powerful. At a meeting you can be made to feel very insecure, stupid and inept because you are the only one to think differently.

If you are the victim of 'mob appeal' at a meeting, here are some suggestions to overcome the situation.

𝔄CTIONS YOU TAKE

☞ *Focus in on a leader*

Sometimes the mob doesn't exist. You may think there is a group of people disagreeing with you, but in fact all you can hear is one voice. Usually one strong person using inclusive language, saying 'we' believe this, or 'we' want that ... But when you consider the whole group, no one else is saying a word. They are just following this leader unquestioning, or this leader could be talking for them without their permission.

There are a number of ways to tackle this leadership position: Say nothing during the meeting, but make a mental note to meet this person on their own later. Defer any decision-making until a further meeting and in the meantime see if you can take this 'leader' to one side to talk to you on a one-to-one basis. Invite them to lunch or coffee where you will have an easier chance of changing their mind. You will then be going a long way to changing the minds of the rest of the group as well.

During the meeting, ask individual people for their views. Check that they all, as individuals, agree with the leader and ask for the reasons why. A lot harder to do, I agree, but the results should be quite staggering, as rarely will a full group of people all agree for the same reasons. The mechanism of asking each individual has the capacity to break through the cohesion of the group.

☞ Bring a buddy

If you know you are going to have a difficult time at a meeting or discussion, ask someone for support before you go in. Then when you run into difficulties they will be a second voice which may produce a third voice in your favour, and so on. Also with a second voice, mob appeal is much harder, if not impossible, to produce. You must, of course, be able to trust the buddy you choose!

☞ Believe in yourself

Do not allow others to make you feel you are wrong. Invite them to prove to you how they have reached their conclusions and decisions. Make them be clear to you, not vice versa. This can be done very meekly as in 'Perhaps I have missed something here, can you explain why you chose to go ahead with this decision, Jack?' (member of the meeting). As in tradition never defend your position against your attacker.

The way to win this argument is to get others to explain their position to you and to explain your strengths to them.

'No one would believe me!' he said.

This story was told to me by a young man whose passion and belief in his product turned around a serious drop in sales to a sales increase of 940 per cent.

It is a good example because it shows the power of a 'false authority' to seduce an audience with simple mob appeal. It also shows how with clear thinking and the correct, credible assistance you can overcome this type of situation.

In 2000, Kealan, our young man, launched a lifestyle medical product with great success. Following this initial launch, the product proved successful with both the medical community and the general public. In fact, the expert authority here was the medical profession as the product had been developed by a medical professional using medical expertise and knowledge.

The product continued to be well prescribed giving overall successful results until, some months later, a media sensationalist story hit the headlines questioning the safety of the product. Notice the media only questioned the safety of the product – they did not give evidence for lack of safety. The media were not medics, but that doesn't matter, because the media, although a 'false authority' in medical matters is very much an 'impressive authority' in society in general. Even though the media couldn't give confirmed evidence against this product, their power lay in their ability to raise fear, uncertainty and doubt in the minds of their readers.

The story took hold in the press. The damage created by the sensationalist media stories lingered in the minds of both physicians and patients alike. The sales of the product began to fall – Kealan was pitched against the very formidable force of the media. There was no use taking them on, or attacking back, as he was fighting force, not facts. The media were not the real authority. Their success lay simply in creating stories with seductive mob appeal.

Kealan decided to combat the situation by using the actions mentioned above. He developed a programme plan with three steps:

Define target audience groups
Identify key messages
Implement specific activities

He wished to achieve three objectives:

Combat negative press with good PR
Rebuild confidence
Increase sales

Focus on the leader

The leader was of course the press itself. So Kealan organised presentations with those journalists who had expressed an interest in his product. His intention was to get them to persuade both the public and their wayward colleagues. If he could convince at least some sections of the press, then positive stories would begin to flow and the negative ones would fade into the background.

Bring a buddy

The keynote speaker at these briefings was the very formidable expert who had helped develop the product. This was essential for rebuilding credibility. This medical doctor was not only capable of overcoming any confusion created by the negative press, she was extremely persuasive in demonstrating the validity and usefulness of the product itself. She had the expertise and knowledge to provide her audience with appropriate scientific backup when recommending the product, with the necessary research details and statistical results.

The audience was impressed. Positive articles began to reappear.

Believe in your ability to succeed

Based on this initial success, Kealan was now convinced he could turn around this negative situation.

He repeated the same process with other target audience groups like medical practitioners, key opinion formers and the general public. Each presentation included the positive input of the medical expert who had developed the product along with other credible medics. There was always time for plenty of interaction and open communication between speakers and audience.

The results were staggering. The media, so negative a few months ago, was now delivering key positive messages across the influential press and broadcast mediums. A steady stream of positive, feature related coverage was generated from November 2001 through to the end of January 2002 and beyond.

And the most astonishing thing of all ... The press was now so impressed with the credibility of Kealan's medical expert that he was inundated with media requests to interview her. What did Kealan do? Due to time constraints he had to limit those interviews to only those key press contacts who had previously expressed a positive interest in his product (revenge is sweet!).

But of course the best result of all was in his sales – a 940 per cent increase.

Remember WHAT to do

1: TRADITION

☺ Acknowledge their position

☺ Ask Wisdom questions to gain information

☺ With this information, use 'yes-and'

☺ List your benefits for new situation

2: POWER OF THE GROUP

☺ Focus on a leader

☺ Bring a buddy

☺ Believe in yourself

2
FUDs – Fear, Uncertainty, Doubt

Death's a breeze … How do I know?
Have you ever seen anyone come back to complain?
STEVE MARTIN IN *LEAP OF FAITH* (1992)

What it is

The acronym FUD (Fear – Uncertainty – Doubt) is attributed to an IBM advertisement of the 1970s. At that time the company ran a publicity billboard campaign directed at corporate IT purchasing managers which read *Nobody ever got fired for buying an IBM*. Just think about it! No evidence is given as to why IBM is the superior product. No comparison is made between IBM and its competitors. The power of the statement is in the fear, uncertainty and doubt it creates. The innuendo it sets up is that no one ever got fired for buying an IBM, but maybe, just maybe, they might have done if they had bought some of the other brands … Connecting the concepts of 'not being fired' and 'buying IBM products' was a clever association. (Just as today Benneton would have us believe, through their thought-provoking advertising, that by buying a Benneton jumper we are in some way making the world a better place!)

But to go back to IBM, the executives didn't have to prove what they were saying. The real punch was that the intended audience could never disprove such a statement. So the audience was left guessing – 'can I take the risk of buying products from other companies. Would they be inferior? Could I lose my job? Perhaps I should play safe with IBM'. Just as in the Steve Martin quote above, the power of these statements lies in the fact that they *cannot* be disproved – although Steve Martin is a lot funnier, I think.

In classical philosophy, this trick is called 'argument from force' but I think the acronym FUD is a much more memorable term and my thanks to IBM for putting it into everyday use.*

FUDs *are so easy*

Inducing fear, uncertainty and doubt is amazingly easy to do and an extremely powerful method of persuasion. It works on the very simple premise that I don't have to prove my point to you. A much greater way of gaining influence over your thinking is to make sure that you cannot *disprove* what I am saying. So you are left in the awkward situation of perhaps not fully believing me, but yet afraid to take the risk of not believing me.

'You'd be nothing without me!' (sound familiar?)

The beauty of this trick is that I don't have to show any logic or evidence for my ideas. As long as I can sow the seed of risk or desire in your mind in such a way that your emotions are stimulated, you may well be enticed to believe me.

Do you buy lottery tickets every week? Don't you find the slogan 'It could be you' so seductive? It is an extremely powerful statement because no one can disprove it and it is a possibility. So millions of people buy tickets and one person wins. The lottery people are very happy indeed.

* IBM *have recently rerun this powerful advertisement, 30 years later – and this time* listing *the evidence to show they are the best.*

The probability of you winning, which is the reality of the situation, is very low indeed. In fact, the odds are stacked entirely against you. Yet, no one likes to think of the cold logic of this situation (certainly not the lottery people) because the seduction of the possibility is so strong and, more importantly, it makes you believe your dreams just might come true.

Or have you ever seen a poor insurance company? Business profits are guaranteed by the number of policy holders who do not have accidents, and who do not become ill. The insurance company, in order to remain a viable business, must ensure that the number of non-claimants is always higher than the number of claimants. Yet, all policy holders take out insurance because they cannot take the risk that they won't need the cover. Fear, uncertainty and/or doubt are the motivating forces behind a lot more than we would like to admit.

How it happens

Do other people get you to carry out actions based on FUDS? Here are some examples:

If I weren't here to help you, you'd never be able to succeed.

If you fall victim to this trick, you may well believe that you cannot be a success on your own. You may believe that your success is dependent on the person who is saying this to you, although they provide absolutely no proof for what they are saying. The power of this statement lies in your belief in it. Perhaps, low self-esteem or a lack of confidence in yourself, or a fear of change keeps you attached to a person or an organisation, because you believe you cannot make it on your own.

But have you ever tried? No? Then, where is the proof that you cannot? Believing in a FUD like this one can paralyse you into not developing your true potential. Other examples of FUDs are:

(a) I'm just putting forward suggestions, it's up to you whether you accept them or not (and of course the responsibility is yours if things go wrong).

Here, the person gives you the responsibility of taking the risk. They put themselves in the clear as regards any decision-making. But remember, if they are putting forward suggestions they should show how valid these suggestions are and what evidence there is for going forward with them. Your ability to accept suggestions is *dependent* on what kind of evidence you are given. If you have no evidence, no decision on acceptance is possible.

(b) I know you are worried about these proposals, but can you take the risk of not carrying them out?

Here, the speaker is forcing you to make a decision based on *fear*, without giving any evidence. They are tricking your emotions into worrying about the possibility of risk or no risk, when you should be looking at what *degree* of risk is involved.

(c) I'll never be able to speak to a large group of people.

(d) It's no use trying to give up smoking, I just won't be able to do it.

Where is the proof for all or any of the above statements? There isn't any given. If you believe them, it is with complete lack of evidence. Your fears, uncertainties and doubts have been hit and you are responding accordingly. You become trapped in your own indecision.

ℬCTIONS YOU TAKE

☞ *Ask for evidence*

If you are the victim of a FUD, to think quickly on your feet, simply ask your opponent for evidence. The less evidence we have the more our decisions rely on risk taking. Evidence and risk are at two opposite ends of the spectrum:

Evidence ....> ————————> Risk

Evidence ————————< ....< Risk

The less evidence you have, the more risk. And conversely, more evidence – less risk. If somebody wants you to do something they must give you the information and the facts, ask them.

For example, responding to:

'I know you are worried about these proposals, but can you take the risk of not carrying them out?'

You might say something like:

'Interesting comment, you are hitting a nerve there, which is why I really need you to quantify the degree of risk you mean, before we carry on.'

𝒯RUE SUCCESS STORY

FUDs you use against yourself:

On starting out on my career as a training consultant in Clear and Critical Thinking *twelve years ago, I had a huge fear of talking* to large groups. My FUDs were: 'if you talk to a large group, you will forget what you want to say' or 'if you talk to a large group your voice will go'. So, what did I do to overcome this false thinking? I played to a higher fear and greater goal – my fear of looking irrational or foolish while building a professional reputation.

What I did was I rang a list of companies introducing my product and myself. When they became interested and said they would like to know more, I suggested the best method would be if I could give a short presentation to a large number of their managers. This sounded appealing to them and it was also very cost effective. So, I made an appointment to give a presentation within the month. That way I had time to prepare and psyche myself up. Backing out was not a possibility as my reputation was far dearer to me than my fear of speaking in public. Having set myself up I had to go through with it. And it worked! I got used to giving lots of presentations and can now do so without a moment's hesitation – I actually enjoy them.

The motto of the story: if your fears are stopping you from doing something that is important or necessary, create a higher goal to strive for and you will eventually forget them.

QUICK
THINKING

Remember WHAT to do

WHEN OTHERS USE FUDs
☺ Ask for evidence
☺ Demand proof

WHEN YOU USE FUDs
☺ Strive for a higher goal

3
ABUSE

> *If you look like your passport photo, you probably need the holiday*

You will probably recognise this trick. I'm afraid we are all guilty of using it at some time – that is, the trick of hitting people's 'emotional buttons' to win an argument. It is so easy and works so beautifully.

WHAT IT IS

When we don't like what someone is saying we tend to shoot the messenger, not the message. In other words, we abuse the speaker, which is a very lazy way of winning the argument, since we don't have to bother with the content of the discussion.

The power of the 'abuse' trick is that, if you fall victim to it, you will get caught up in the confusion of associating 'ego' with 'issue'. This is very powerful as it diverts the attention of the victim. When you are on the receiving end of this, it can be totally debilitating. This type of trigger diverts your clear thinking away from your original goal and the logical conclusion you are trying to reach. Instead, your focus becomes completely centred on your ego and its safety.

This is doubly dangerous because a lot of times when people fall into this trap they feel so good at having defended themselves from attack, that they totally fail to see they have lost the argument and will fail to reach their goal.

---

*H*OW IT HAPPENS

A wonderful example told to me by some British politicians illustrates this point beautifully.

A Labour councillor was in the middle of delivering a very clear and concise proposal on education policy, when suddenly a Conservative jumped up shouting 'what would you know about education, you're not educated yourself?' At which point all the Labour man's colleagues rose en masse protesting the vulgarity of such a statement. This, of course, played wonderfully into the Conservative's plan, for in the mayhem the clever ideas of the Labour councillor were completely forgotten!

You may think it is only politicians who play like this, unfortunately the practice is widespread. How many times with friends and family have you attacked the person, and not the problem? And how many times has this made a discussion descend into a full-blown argument?

Sometimes, it is incredibly difficult to combat this particular trick as its effect is almost instantaneous. And when the accuser is able to tap into a specific trait in your ego and hit it with force, then you must seriously understand what is going on to be able to think quickly on your feet and not be diverted.

An example of hitting into a specific trait of the ego like this was told to me by a young woman attending one of my training courses. She told me of her experience at a recent meeting:

I was arguing my point very clearly and with some force. I was

*quite happy that I knew my stuff and I was able to put my mes-
sage across like the best of them. Then suddenly, my colleague,
John, looked me in the eye and said, 'Sarah, you're always on the
defensive'.*

  *'No, I'm not,' I replied far too quickly, because by saying this
at that moment, I became defensive. This of course, easily proved
his point. My argument was completely weakened and I found it
very difficult to regain credibility within the group.*

Oh dear! All of us have the same tendency as Sarah. When our
ego is hit or hurt we will immediately run to its defence. Not
being defensive was very important to Sarah. That was her
particular button and when pressed, she fell into the trap of
saving her ego. This is what people can do to you in a discussion. If they don't like what you are saying, they can very
cleverly (like John) attack a certain trait in your ego that they
know you will rush to defend. And if you fall for this trick, they
will achieve the result they are looking for which is to divert
your attention away from the issue. In addition, by doing so, if
they can unnerve your confidence and lessen your credibility
within the group, they will ensure that your goal (the one they
never wanted) will not be realised.

ACTIONS YOU TAKE

The first thing to realise if you are the victim of the trick of
'argument abuse' is that the person attacking you is in a very
weak position indeed. What I have found most of all, while
teaching this type of 'thinking on your feet' during the past
twelve years, is that when I come to recognise a trick (and
especially this one) I can become much more powerful in getting what I want. Instead of reacting and going into the trap,

once I recognise it for what it is, I think, 'how wonderful, if the other party is reduced to this level of thinking, they must have absolutely no proof or evidence for what they are saying. So, in fact, I am stronger than they are here and this gives me a very powerful psychological advantage'.

You can think the same way. If your opponent had any evidence for a counter argument, they could simply give it. By being reduced to this kind of abuse, it is a clear indication that they haven't. They have no proof to argue against you so the only thing they can do is to divert your attention instead. This knowledge should make you feel more powerful, not more confused.

☞ *Always get back to the issue*

If you feel yourself becoming emotional during an argument STOP, even for a split second – this is so you can remain calm. Some people however may find it hard to stop, precisely because they are emotional, but focus is the key here, and determination. You won't always succeed at being unemotional about everything, but when the situation or topic is really important to you, remember what the point is you are trying to get across and then never forget it. Prepare well for a difficult meeting so that you will be less likely to stray off the point. Do not let others divert you. Always bring the conversation back to that issue.

There are several ways you can do this:

☞ *Simply ignore the abuse (remember Napoleon's famous saying 'I never interrupt my enemy when he is making a mistake' [at least that's how you can justify your silence to others later]).*

☞ Use humour: 'I see I'm not flavour of the month. However, the point is …'

☞ Defer it: 'we can discuss that later, the point now is …'

No matter how you deal with the situation, always get back to the issue.

Never allow abuse to divert your thinking. *Quick Thinking on your Feet* is not about being assertive. You do not have to say anything. In fact standing up for yourself may well mean you will go off the point. Remember not to fall into the feel-good factor trap. If you haven't reached your goal, no matter how good you feel, you have failed.

To reach that goal, take a deep breath, smile and carry on with clear direction towards what you want to achieve – without diverting.

---

*T*RUE SUCCESS STORY

Anne found the task of dealing with Mike very difficult indeed. Yet, the two of them had to meet frequently as Anne was the management representative and Mike the trade union official for their particular company. They often had disputes – or lively discussions as Mike called them – which always made Anne feel extremely uncomfortable. No matter how hard she tried, Anne always came away from these meetings feeling very angry or upset about what had happened. She certainly did not feel in control of any meeting they had been through. Then she began to learn about the techniques of thinking on your feet. She attended one of my sessions on the ten tricks of manipulation and finally began to understand that she was being tricked by false and manipulative reasoning. Usually, because she couldn't stand up to aggressive, and sometimes abusive, comments.

Soon after one particular session on our training programme, Anne had reason for a confrontation with Mike over a particularly nasty industrial relations issue. This problem had become so serious that a meeting was called with senior union and management personnel, where both Anne and Mike were told to present their case. The meeting was scheduled for 2 p.m. on a Monday afternoon.

Shortly before the meeting, Mike and Anne were in the corridor awaiting the others. Mike began his usual scenario of blaming and bullying Anne. This time Anne looked him straight in the eye, repeated what he had just said and replied, 'That's a false argument' (notice she didn't need the full title of the trick used).

Mike looked at her and said 'I don't want any of that psychological bullshit!'

Anne remained calm, ignoring the remark, she smiled sweetly and walked away. She felt in control. Before this, she would have reacted and become emotional at such an outburst. But now, realising this was a diversionary tactic, she was able to break a habit with this particular person. Even though it was difficult, she remained confident.

They went into the meeting-room and joined the others. To her surprise, Mike was very subdued at the meeting. He allowed Anne to make her case without interruption. All points were discussed and openly debated and satisfactory conclusions for all were reached. What happened? Anne believes that once she had shown she would no longer react to abusive tricks in argument, Mike could not use them. This is an important point to note. Because people say it is habit-forming to react emotionally in argument, they believe they cannot *change. But as it is habit-forming to react to such tricks, it is also habit-forming for the trickster to know who they can use these tricks with – and who they cannot. If, like Anne, you stand up to such a person, even once, they will change their behaviour, because part of their shrewdness in using this trick is to know who they can succeed with. The last thing they will risk is public humiliation.* Using 'abuse' will only work if the victim falls into the trap. *Once you have the courage to stand firm and show you will not do so (even that once), it becomes more frightening for the perpetrator to try again.*

You will be happy to know that Anne and Mike now have a satisfactory, professional relationship.

QUICK
THINKING

Remember WHAT to do

☺ Use humour

☺ Defer to later

☺ Remember the mantra: ALWAYS GET BACK TO
THE ISSUE

4
STEREOTYPING

> When I was younger, I hated going to weddings. All my aunts and grand-
> motherly types used to come up to me, poke me in the ribs and say: 'You're
> next, you're next ...'
>
> I got them to stop though ... How? ... I started doing the same thing
> to them at funerals ...

WHAT IT IS

I hope you enjoyed that joke. Don't you just love it when you
can throw the attack right back at them?

Stereotyping is quite similar to abuse. As a trick, it has the
same impact, that is to divert your attention away from the
issue and on to your ego. It differs from abuse in that it is not a
specific trait of your ego that is being attacked, instead, it is
what or who you are. The implication is that because you are a
man, woman, manager, worker, engineer, actress or whatever
... you couldn't possibly know what you are talking about. If
you fall victim to this trick you will start defending yourself as
a man, woman, etc. ... instead of defending the particular point
you are trying to make.

HOW IT HAPPENS

Where there is lack of trust and cynicism
As with abuse, this occurs when others do not want to listen to
the content of your argument, and hope to quickly brush you
aside. It can often be a symptom of extreme lack of trust like

when relations in a company have broken down. Management try to put forward ideas to workers, and instead of listening to the content of what is proposed, the ideas are quickly branded as 'only corporate speak'. Or vice versa, staff proposals are rubbished as 'only out for themselves'. Clear thinking is completely stymied by the sourness of the experience.

When change is being introduced

Other instances of stereotyping are when new ideas are being put forward. This is particularly relevant for people trying to start a new business, or sell a new product or change to a new career. Others will often argue that you are too old, young, under experienced, *over* experienced, a man, a woman … the list is endless.

With wrong mental attitude

Of course, you can also quite expertly do this to yourself. You might stereotype *yourself*, as being too old, young, poor, shy … again the list is endless, when you are afraid to take on a new challenge. How many times have you used the phrase 'I'm no good at …'? Remember, if you put limitations on yourself, you will succeed at being limited. The choice is yours.

On the very large scale stereotyping can descend into a very extreme, toxic type of groupthink. In Germany during the Second World War, and more recently Rwanda and Bosnia millions of people were murdered because of their race. On a small scale, it is just as toxic, paralysing individuals from developing both themselves and those around them to stretch their potential and broaden their horizons.

☞ *Listen to each other*

In a very general sense, the first way to overcome stereotyping between any groups or individuals is to *listen* to each other. No matter how hard this is, allow each side to talk through their ideas without interruption and *listen for the logic and common sense* in what they are saying. Always concentrate on issue, not ego. Do not dismiss others or allow yourself to be dismissed. Search for core points, common goals, and compatible suggestions that can benefit *both sides* to move forward. If the situation is particularly serious, a mediator is a good idea.

☞ *Gain trust first*

It is not a good idea to try to convince someone who doesn't trust you. The other person(s) will tend to twist and turn what you thought were great ideas and brilliant arguments into something you may not even recognise. This is because they are not listening to your words, they are trying to evaluate them through their own belief screen of mistrust. Even if they do see a good idea, they still might not accept it as they may be thinking – 'they are only doing this to line their own pockets, they are only saying this now, it won't last …' I have seen many brilliant ideas get destroyed because of this type of situation.

The simple answer here is to make sure there is some trust in the relationship before you meet for discussion. Being clever on your feet when there is no trust may only aggravate the situation and make the other party feel weaker. J. A. Conger, a leading guru on 'leadership' and who has written a wonderful article called 'The Necessary Art of Persuasion' (*Harvard Busi-*

ness Review May/June 1998) defines the equation of good persuasion as 'Expertise + Relationship'. In other words, no matter how expert you might think you are, if you do not have a good relationship with those you are trying to convince, they won't believe a word you are saying – or worse still they may distort your ideas to your disadvantage.

Build/Repair the relationship *first*, then come in with your expertise.

☞ *Do not let people dismiss you*

When you are putting forward newness or change people may often dismiss you and your ability to succeed. I work quite a lot with women starting up their own businesses, both in Ireland and America, and it seems to be, in at least 90 per cent of cases, that these women have suffered some form of stereotyping.

People would say:

> Women have never succeeded in that field before, it is going to be very difficult for you.

> Instead of starting up in financial consulting, why don't you open a flower shop?

> Being a woman, no bank will ever give you the finances (some women did find this one difficult, but overcame all obstacles and got that money).

Remember, when you are stereotyped, this is not *your* problem or perception, but that of your attacker. The reason I say this is that you have nothing to prove to anyone, and therefore you do not even need to respond to this stereotyping. Smile sweetly. You should know that as a woman (or man), setting up your own business, you know what you are doing and you are well capable of doing it. If someone else does not know that, then you will just have to show them as you succeed throughout the years.

☞ *Have a positive mental attitude*
Be careful of your own mental attitude and of stereotyping yourself!

If you do not conform to the status quo, count it as a bonus, you will be a novelty and stand above all the others.

If you are stereotyping yourself as being too old, young, tall, small … change this negative perception into a positive. For example:

'I can't go for that job, I am too old' (assumption old is bad) *change this to*

'I can go for that job, as I have a wealth of experience' (old is good).

The present situation is the same – you are still a person of a certain age – but your perception is making it good or bad.

Remember life is a gift, that is why they call it *the present* – do what you want now!

𝒯RUE SUCCESS STORY

A revenue commissioner, Joe, was used to being stereotyped very negatively by people who didn't want to consider too deeply what he was asking them to do. However, one meeting stands out in his memory as being very gruelling.

Seated around the table in the boardroom of a particularly difficult client, six company men and Joe were reading a report of recommendations. Joe had devised these in an attempt to save the enterprise.

However, some time into reading through the complex report, one of the men looked Joe, straight in the eye, and said 'Of course, Joe, I think we can see your arrogance as a revenue official shining right through here.'

What would you do if you were Joe? Lesser mortals might react very strongly to such an attack. Perhaps insult the person back and do even more damage.

Joe listened very calmly and asked the man quite politely where he saw the arrogance within the report. Was it on page three, at paragraph four, etc? In this way he showed very clearly that the problem this man had was with a recommendation in the report, and not with Joe himself.

Joe was following the mantra – always get back to the issue – something you should remember when any form of abuse occurs.

Joe then discovered the problem recommendation, discussed it in greater detail, and allayed the fears that the company had about it.

The meeting ended very agreeably.

QUICK
THINKING

Remember WHAT to do

☺ Listen to each other

☺ Gain trust first

☺ Do not let people dismiss you

☺ Have a positive mental attitude

☺ Always get back to the issue

5

YOU'RE WRONG, SO I'M RIGHT

WHAT IT IS

This is probably the most complicated trick of all. It can be devastating and completely shatter your confidence, especially if you are assaulted with this trick when you are presenting your ideas in front of a group of people.

The power of this manipulation is to confuse the two thinking skills of analysis and production. Let's look first at 'analysis'. At this moment you are analysing what you are reading. You are asking yourself if what you have read in this book so far makes sense. You may have agreed with some of the things I have said and you may strongly disagree with others. Or you may have questions you would like to ask me to clarify some points you would like to hear more on. This is your brain at work analysing, evaluating and making judgements on the information it is receiving. Some people are experts at analysis. They can spot immediately if someone has a good or bad argument. They can see the flaws in the argument when someone is trying to prove that they have a good idea, or that what they are saying is right. And all of this they can do, simply by listening and analysing what is being said.

This is indeed a great skill. But it doesn't produce any ideas of its own. What you may have done is an expert analysis, but that is where it ends. It cannot follow that because you can analyse well, what you then produce is better than me. In my book example, your expertise is in being able to dismantle my information, but it doesn't follow that because you can analyse well, that you can produce a better book. (It may well be true, of course and in fact it is a great possibility, but it is still not a logical progression ...)

Analysis and production are two different thinking skills. Because a person is good at analysis, it doesn't mean that they can actually produce anything. To produce ideas requires creative thinking. Creative thinking comes up with new ideas, its skill is in seeing the world in new and exciting ways – it changes old concepts into new actions. Instead of analysing what is already there, it changes it and moulds it into something new.

𝓗OW IT HAPPENS

This is how this trick might happen to you, particularly in a work context. In fact, this manipulation is so serious that some people have told me they have lost contracts and important deals by not spotting this one soon enough.

Imagine you are giving an important presentation to some of your colleagues or an outside agency / client. Your audience is listening intently to you and analysing your arguments. You are going through a series of reasons why you think it is a good idea to go ahead with this new product, for example, or to introduce this new service.

What a *PRAT*

There is someone in the audience who doesn't want this new change, but they have no solid argument of their own to stop it being introduced. So they listen very earnestly to you and as you give your list of reasons, they will suddenly stop you and say something like 'hold on a minute, those figures on page 3, they're wrong. Can we go back to those, because I know for a fact they are incorrect'. (I am assuming these figures *are* wrong but also that they are not the central core of your argument.)

This act alone is enough to shatter confidence. To be shown up for some error, no matter how small, in front of other people is a humiliating experience and can confuse us and make us lose any ground we may have gained with the group.

What can also happen now that everyone's attention has been drawn to the fact that there is a mistake in the figures on page 3, is that an awful atmosphere may be creeping around the room and people may be thinking 'Well, if she can't even get the figures right on page three, goodness knows how valid the rest of this is' even though no one has yet heard the rest of the presentation. This is the damage that can be done. Even without any further analysis of the rest of an argument – which may be excellent – people are now having doubts, and may not want to hear any more.

If your accuser sees that he is gaining some recognition for doing this, he may continue with more confidence 'well, we can see that these figures don't add up, and really I don't think it is possible to prove that this new product will work for us. In fact I have always thought this should not be a runner for us. I think it is a bad idea'.

Where is his *proof* that this is a bad idea? There is none. If you look at the small diagram below showing the difference between 'analysis' and 'production' you will see that the production box is entirely empty.

There is not one reason in the production box to show why your idea is wrong, all your accuser has done is to analyse one of the reasons that you use to try to prove your case. In finding fault it proves only that you are not right. However, it does not follow from this that you are wrong.

'Not right' does not mean 'wrong'

Your accuser has produced no ideas to prove you are wrong. All he has done is to show a flaw in your argument that shows you are not able to prove you are right. Being 'not right' doesn't mean you are 'wrong'. It may simply mean you don't have a strong enough argument to prove that you are right. You may be very right, it's just that part of your argument is not good. Attacking part of your argument does not prove that your whole idea is worthless. Just because *you* make a mistake does not mean that *they* are right.

ANALYSIS	PRODUCTION
√Good Reason *Reason [*wrong figures*] √Good Reason √Good Reason √Good Reason	
You are not right *does not equal* **you are wrong**	

* *Even if there is a flaw, not right does not equal wrong*

However, that is how this type of attack might make you feel – worthless. You may doubt yourself and other people in the room may be very concerned as well about the viability of your work. There is a way to overcome this though so do not fret.

ℋCTIONS YOU TAKE

REMEMBER **PRAT**

☞**P** – *Prepare well*

To avoid this attack happening in the first place it is a good idea to be very well prepared. Whether you are showing a business plan, sales products, or looking for a loan from the bank, it is a good idea to ensure no one *can* attack your figures or find fault with your arguments by making sure they are well thought through and well checked.

It is important to do this, because there is a grain of truth to feeling less confident about someone who doesn't seem to be well prepared. We wonder 'if they are that sloppy about their facts and figures, maybe the rest is no good'. Unfortunately that has a ring of truth about it. So, be well prepared.

☞**R** – *Remain calm*

However, even if well prepared, we are after all human, and we will make some mistakes. If this happens, the first thing to remember is remain calm. The one positive point to never forget here is that they are listening to you. That is a wonderful privilege. The amount of people who go to presentations and fall asleep, talk to others, do other work and not listen is phenomenal. So, if you have them listening to you that is a very positive acknowledgement of the importance of your work.

☞A – *Acknowledge the point*

The worse thing that can happen when someone points out a mistake is denial. The speaker might say, those figures aren't important or argue against the attacker and so get caught up in a very downward spiral. The easiest thing to do is to acknowledge yes, these figures are in fact incorrect. 'Well spotted,' you might say, 'Yes you are absolutely correct. Thank you for pointing that out. I will get someone back at the office to update those corrections immediately. For the moment, I would like to park them, so we can continue with the excellent analysis you are giving to my work. I would appreciate your judgement on the rest of the arguments I am putting forward. For example, you will see I have four other points here. What do you think of …?'

☞T – *Take back control*

Now you have their attention very firmly back onto developing your ideas. I am assuming that each new reason they meet (as in the diagram on page 81) they will agree with.* Then you can say 'Well now that we have agreed with all of these reasons, I think that when we reintroduce the new corrected figures to complement these reasons, we will have a *stronger* product than I anticipated. And that, Jim (attacker), is thanks to you spotting that mistake on page 3. Well done and thank you for your valuable contribution to the project …'

Won't you just feel great?

By the way, if lots of your reasons are wrong, then someone pointing this out, is not using a trick. In fact, they are doing both you and your company a great service. If the information as a whole, or the many reasons you are citing as evidence, are incorrect, then you are very ill prepared and I believe, should not be giving a presentation at all.

Deirdre wanted a colleague to read her report and act on the recommendations she had written in it.

He did not want to do this, but had no real argument against her. They met and she gave him her work. As she handed it over, she noticed that her secretary had typed 31 November 2000 on the front cover of the report. (As we all know this date doesn't exist.) Her colleague noticed this too.

He flung the report back at her saying, 'well, if you can't even get the date right on the report, how am I supposed to believe what is inside it?'

This could have meant disaster. She would never be able to get him to read her arguments and be convinced by them.

But she didn't flinch. She caught his comment instantly and said 'My goodness, you know I have shown this report to several people, and none of them noticed it had the wrong date on it. What a marvellous eye you have for detail. You most definitely must read this report for me now, as I really think you are the only one I can trust to make an informed and complete judgement on this information'.

He trotted off happily, with the report under his arm. And yes, he did read it (a little bit of flattery always helps).

Robert's story

As a consultant, Robert was asked to look at the human resources aspect of a retail business. The results suggested that the company was undergoing a period of high staff turnover, declining labour productivity, and just a general decline in efficiencies. A written report was sent to the company for their evaluation. Because of that report a meet-

ing was scheduled at a time mutually agreed by him and the company to discuss the content of that document.

He produced an agenda which he sent to the company for approval and it was agreed by all. He arrived for the meeting on time, the others were late – the managing director by thirty minutes, others by ten.

They exchanged greetings and then he again asked for agreement as to the agenda for the meeting. He gave an outline for the reason for the meeting. Within two minutes of starting the first agenda topic, he was interrupted by a comment of 'Let's talk about your figures, because they really concern me – your figures are wrong'.

'Which figures in particular are we talking about?' he asked.

'These figures,' the MD pointed, 'your figures on labour productivity are wrong.'

He replied, 'what should they be?'

To which the reply was 'we certainly don't have declining productivity. Productivity has increased', and to justify that she said, 'look our revenue has increased'.

His response, 'Ok, well maybe my figures are wrong, I will go back and check'.

'Good,' she said.

For the remainder of the meeting, each time he tried to work through the agenda, he would, every now and again, be interrupted by something that was not related to that particular agenda item. He was beginning to think this might be a strategy to derail him. Each time it happened he would say 'Ok, that's obviously an important point to look at, it is not however this particular agenda item, let's look at it later so we can do full justice to these agenda items now' (the ones they had agreed on at the beginning of the meeting).

By now with all the interruptions, they had got to a point where the MD needed to leave. She had already turned up thirty minutes late and only stayed an hour. The meeting ended with her suggestion that she give him written feedback on his work later 'as we haven't read it all yet properly,' she said. ('Ok, so I'm going to be attacked some more,' he thought.)

A week later they sent him a three-page email full of criticism. At times, it was bordering on pettiness. The email ended with 'we need you to read this and understand that when you come in for our next meeting, this project will have to be put back on track' (his fault again – his project off track? This was news to him). He was unsettled. He knew the next meeting would be confrontational. The company was going to want to defend itself.

He was getting fed up with this, he felt it was becoming a waste of his time.

However, before the meeting, he worked very hard on trying to see the other point of view. He was advised to go in with someone else who was not so emotionally involved in the situation. He intended to do this. The company told him he would get a week to prepare. He didn't.

The meeting was scheduled for Monday, but he only got this information on Friday morning – so he had to go on his own.

He walked into the meeting at 9.30 a.m. very aware that he was going to be confronted. He power-dressed, dark suit, white shirt, red tie. He wanted them to understand that he was here to do proper business, and that he was confident in what he was doing. He arrived on time. The MD was caught up with an emergency, so he and the other person at the meeting, a company employee, Thomas, had to start without her. Robert came in very upbeat, not meek. They started their meeting at 9.40 a.m. Thomas immediately said 'let's get to labour *productivity figures, I need you to defend your figures'.*

Robert worked through his methodology for calculating labour productivity. Thomas sat there – silence.

'OK,' he said, 'I need you to defend your statement that we are not as efficient as we were'.

He worked through this again as above. More silence.

Then a half-hearted stab at another area of criticism. But Thomas' language was milder, no longer, 'I need you to defend' ... but more simply 'what about these ...?'

At this point the MD walked in.

Thomas said, 'Robert has been through some labour productivity and efficiencies. Maybe Robert, you could recount that for Jane.'

He did that.

Silence.

'OK,' Jane said and continued, 'well, you should have explained in your report how you got the figures. You should have pointed out that we were not comparing like with like in our estimates and therefore were mistaken'.

He had done that. She grudgingly accepted that his figures were correct. It felt good. He was now very confident in proceeding with the meeting.

At the end of the meeting, Jane, the MD, asked him if he had been pleased with the meeting. He replied that yes, he did feel happy about where his work was coming from. He felt confident about what he was doing, how he was doing it and where he was planning to take the project.

'I suppose the real question,' he said, 'is has this meeting been good for you, as you appeared to have some issues with the project?'

To which the reply was 'Well, I just don't like people who criticise and don't have their figures right, it really gets my back up.'

He was flabbergasted. 'Excuse me if I sound a little bit confused,' he said, 'but I thought we had clarified that my figures were correct, have I misunderstood?'

'Well, maybe your figures are right, it's just the way that you say it ...' she said.

Remember Robert's story and remember **PRAT** – Prepare: Remain calm: Acknowledge: Take back control.

QUICK THINKING

Remember WHAT to do

Just think of the acronym PRAT, because that is what they usually are.

🙂 P – Prepare well

🙂 R – Remain calm

🙂 A – Acknowledge the point

🙂 T – Take back control

6
FALSE CAUSE

The easiest way to bully, cause blame or make people feel guilty is to interject a 'false cause' into a discussion. This makes the listener feel at fault for some wrongdoing even though there is no proof given that they have made a mistake or done anything incorrect. This trick can totally cloud the judgement of the most ardent clear thinker.

WHAT IT IS

The way 'false cause' works is as follows:

In our thinking, there are two ways in which events may be linked, either as a sequence or as a cause. An example of a sequence of 'A then B' is in 'today then tomorrow' (1). An example of two causal events of 'A then B' is in 'rain, then wet streets' (2).

In both instances, A occurs first and B follows, but in the first example (1) above of 'today then tomorrow' what we have is only a sequence. We could never say that today *causes* tomorrow. Tomorrow simply *follows* today, it is not caused by it. However, in case of the rain and wet streets (2) above, the rain does come first, and also *causes* the streets to become wet. Sequence only in example (1), sequence plus cause in example (2).

When someone uses 'false cause' they transform a simple sequence into a cause with absolutely no evidence.

For example, say a problem arises at work or at home and someone rushes up to you shouting, in an agitated state: 'I knew we shouldn't have made that decision three months ago. Look what's happened now!' (the more dramatic the better).

What if they continue with 'of course, *I* never wanted us to do this in the first place, I said we should hold off, but would you listen? No, you wanted to go ahead. It was your pet project and *you* said you could handle anything that would happen ... Can you handle this now?'

How are you feeling? Do you want to defend yourself? Is your natural inclination to justify your decision? Are you feeling a little insecure? If you are feeling in any way defensive, responsible or lacking in confidence then you have fallen for this trick.

The brilliance of this trick is to produce guilt in the mind of the listener so that instead of hearing a simple sequence they will see a cause, and the greater the guilt the more they will think they are responsible and at fault.

But go back over the two original sentences 'I knew we shouldn't have made that decision three months ago. Look what's happened now', and you will see there is no causal connection given between the two events. All you know is that a decision was made three months ago and there is a problem now. So what! There is no evidence that your decision *caused* this problem. You have only two statements of fact. A decision was made. A problem has arisen. Your own defensiveness has made you make the leap that one *caused* the other. The speaker never said this. They simply used a mind game of implying that one was responsible for the other. Your own guilt and lack of confidence does the rest.

This is a very serious trick and one where *esprit d'escalier* or 'staircase wit' comes to us in full force – usually in the middle of the night, when you can suddenly bolt up in your bed realising 'but that had nothing to do with me!'

When this trick is successful the victim usually says something like 'ok, we have a problem, but let's concentrate on resolving it now'. This is wrong, it assumes you *are* responsible. Or, 'I wasn't 100 per cent sure of my decision at the time, but I never thought this would happen'. Again wrong, it assumes responsibility. This trick is used extensively in bullying, accusation and inflicting blame. However, it can be overcome very simply.

𝕬CTIONS YOU TAKE

If a problem arises and you are accused of being responsible, the first thing to do is *listen calmly and carefully*. If you feel doubtful, guilty or confused about what you have done as someone accuses you of incompetence or lack of judgement, hold on for dear life to your emotions. Remain calm and simply ask them for proof of the accusation.

For instance in the above case of your decision causing the current problem – you could say something like:

'That's interesting, how do you make the connection between these two events?' (said *very* calmly).

And, if you really want to show off, you could add 'of course I can see the sequence between the events, but where is the cause?'

I am assuming that you are *not* at fault here, of course. If the speaker has proof that you *are* responsible, then they are not using the trick of 'false cause' and you are in deep trouble. Admit it and take the positive step of finding creative solutions. Grovelling also helps a lot here too.

⁊RUE SUCCESS STORY

Mark is a maths teacher in a college catering for fifteen to seventeen year olds. At a certain time, there was industrial unrest in the school and the teachers decided to go out on short one- and two-day lightening strikes. Only a total of four days was taken during the months of February and March in the particular year of unrest. The following September there was a serious drop in the number of students.

A meeting was called, during which one teacher stood up and made a very impassioned speech about how he knew they should never have gone out on strike. 'Look at the damage the strike has caused,' he said.

Because, they were all feeling so guilty about having gone out on strike, everyone in the room was transfixed. No one thought to ask, 'is there a valid connection between the strike and the drop in numbers?'

Mark told me afterwards that when they did look into the matter in more detail, they found there were several reasons for the drop in student intake including a change in county boundaries, shifts in demographics and new school in the area. As it turned out the strike had, in fact, not been the cause of the drop in student numbers. Armed with this new information the teachers, with the school management, were able to make decisions to attract greater numbers of students for future years.

What is interesting in this story, and what made Mark very aware of this trick for the future was that he saw at first hand how an intelligent group of people, because of guilt, become powerless to think clearly when confronted by this particular form of manipulation. It is very powerful and hits the emotions very hard indeed.

Remember WHAT to do

☺ Remain calm
☺ Listen carefully
☺ Never justify yourself
☺ Ask the accuser how they make the causal connection

7
PLAYING WITH WORDS

> *My idea of housework is to sweep the room with a glance*

WHAT IT IS

To describe the trick of 'playing with words' let me ask you what you think of the following argument.

(If) only man is a rational animal
(And) no woman is a man
(Therefore) no woman is rational.

Correct, boys? Finally, they say, we have proof … Believe it or not, girls, the logic of this argument *is* correct. If it is only man who is rational, and no woman *is* a man, then it has to follow that no woman is rational. However, the trick as we can see is that we are being seduced by the logic, how the words are connected together, while ignoring the meaning of the word 'man' and how it changes through the argument.

When people play with words each sentence or statement may be correct, but put together the argument isn't true. As in the example above, even if 'only man is a rational animal' is true, and 'no woman is a man' is true … it cannot follow that 'no woman is rational' because the meaning of the word 'man' is not the same in each statement. 'Man' in the first statement equals 'human race' or 'mankind', the collective noun for men and women, while 'man' in the second statement equals 'male species' only.

Logic the great seducer

When this trick is used in an everyday context, it is of course done in a far more sophisticated way than in the amusing short argument above. Seducing by logic is the age-old trick of creating a wonderful logical web of an argument that is so convincing you would be a fool to disagree with the conclusion. When you are a victim of this trick, what you hear may sound fine, but you still may have an uneasy feeling about how true it is. As in the famous line from the experienced salesperson 'Remember, Mr Jones, you are not buying this product, you are investing in it.' The reality of the situation however, is that you are parting with your money, being told you are investing rather than buying may just ease the pain.

In a work situation, you may find this in report writing. The report writer may argue that all his points make sense but you still don't feel it adds up. He may argue that if you agree with all his points in the report (which you do) then you are contradicting yourself if you don't agree with his conclusion. If this works, you begin to feel you may be logically incoherent and agree with him to save face.

Vision: a great inspiration

'Playing with words' is often commonly used when dealing with concepts. Concepts are nebulous thoughts that you can't actually analyse into a definite idea, but you can understand them very well, like 'beauty', 'truth', 'change', 'progress'. We all understand these concepts but if asked to define 'beauty' or 'progress' for example, we can only give our own subjective evaluation that will differ from person to person.

The chief executive inspiring his employees to 'change' to 'progress' may have definite ideas on how he wants the company to run. Whether or not these ideas are in fact progressive and will bring about constructive change may well be in dispute and only time may tell if they are in fact any good. Everyone may go home on Friday evening delighted after a gung-ho speech on how the company has to progress and embrace change enthusiastically ... but will everyone leave the room with the same understanding of what has been communicated and come back on Monday and used the same 'path to progress'? The reality is they will probably come back and fight about how it all is to be done.

Danger words

Every organisation, business, home, political party has danger words. These are words I describe as having different meanings for different people. Yet, we all use them as if they have one meaning only. You will know these words in your own lives and it would be a good idea to take note of them in your workbook.

These words can cause great manipulation and resentment. For example, in my own work area of training, a danger word we have is 'empowerment'. Empowerment is a word used to motivate people to stretch their talents and develop their potential. Used in a sincere way, as it is most often used, it is wholly believed in and acted on by most responsible organisations. Workers are encouraged to become empowered in the tasks they carry out in their jobs; taking on more responsibility, making more decisions and the like. The idea is that this gives a sense of well being and extra confidence in the workplace. However, the logic sounds terrific, and it should be a great idea, but sometimes empowerment in reality can feel like responsibility without reward. Rather than feeling empowered, people complain of being taken advantage of. They say that more work is 'dumped on' with no extra value to themselves.

Jargon

This one is simple – don't use it. Jargon is only understood by people who are already part of the same small tight-knit community of users. That is why it is best to use your jargon only with your fellow users. If you want to alienate everyone else by using words they don't understand then go ahead. But you will find you cannot communicate with your audience. You may well 'blind them with science' and feel very impressive, but the down side is that they won't be able to understand a word you say. Worse still, they may be afraid to tell you.

ACTIONS YOU TAKE

There is a very simple way of dealing with this manipulation factor and it can be summed up in three words: check for clarity.

☞ Ask for meaning

If you think that the logic of an argument sounds great, but you still feel uneasy or confused, ask the speaker to clarify the meaning of the words they are using. Likewise, you could question the meaning of the words yourself. 'Of course, we all believe in progress, but in what way will this particular idea help us to increase our sales targets? Or, 'yes, change is part of everyday life now, and rapid change in particular, but how will this idea make us change for the better? What will we gain, where and how?' The same with a report. Never accept a report with vague meaning. Remember people need to be able to *understand* what is being written, not have to *interpret* it.

☞ Clarify your own meaning

If you feel inspired by wise statements or flashy advertising, make sure you clarify the meaning of these phrases/images within your own life. Asking 'why?' five times is an established training tool that may help you to do this. For example, we see lots of advertising today inspiring people to change their careers. You may think you feel inspired to change your career, but using the 'five whys' may clarify this thinking.

I feel inspired to change my career.	**Why?**
Because I'm bored with my job.	**Why?**
Because I have too little to do everyday.	**Why?**
Because nobody gives me anything.	**Why?**
Because I never ask them.	**Why?**
Because they all seem so busy ... I'm afraid to ...	

Solution: Find someone you can trust to give you some extra work which will make your day more interesting *and* everyone else's less hectic.

Notice by the third 'why?' the real problem was emerging – you had too little to do. You didn't hate your career choice (in fact you may have chosen it very earnestly). What you needed was more of it not less. So changing career would not have been the right action to take here.

☞ Avoid jargon

If you are communicating ideas to other people, it is best to avoid jargon no matter how terrific it sounds. If you are a consultant, telling people you can devise 'adaptation tools', 'test diversity systems' and 'message point criteria' for them, you may sound wonderful and they may find you impressive. But if no one can understand what you mean you may have a difficult time in securing a client. This happened to a friend of mine recently. A US marketing consultant wanted to promote their work in the United States. My friend said he was very impressed by the consultant and her credentials were very good, but unfortunately he simply couldn't understand her. He has now enlisted the services of a different company. 'We can talk,' he says. Remember, KISS is quite effective for most normal people – 'keep it simple, stupid'.

☞ Say it another way

If you are on the receiving end of jargon – and you want to continue the relationship – a simple technique to achieve clarity is to ask the speaker to 'say it another way'. For example, 'a people carrier' said another way is 'a large automobile capable of carrying six to eight people. 'Earth defying fossil treatment' is a great shampoo and so on. If you don't understand, simply ask them to say it another way. Remember the onus to communicate effectively is on the speaker not you.

TRUE SUCCESS STORY

There are many funny anecdotes for this particular trick. Here are two short ones. One is a story against myself. I will tell you that one first.

A few years ago (before I had the wonderful sales and marketing manager who works with me now, Loretto Mara), I wanted to run a one-day seminar on 'Clear Thinking' for the general public. I placed an advertisement on the back page of The Irish Times. *The seminar was to run at the beginning of April, and thinking I was extremely clever I thought up the caption* Spring clean your mind *giving the details of the seminar with location and short content below it. To my horror, I received no phone calls requesting information about the seminar – but I got tons from 'dry cleaners' asking about my service. They thought it was some sort of new cleaning device that I was demonstrating. It was an expensive blunder. The advertisement had cost me £600. Luckily,* The Irish Times *had also made a mistake – a small typographical error. For this reason, they said they would run the advertisement free for a second day. I was very clear the next day. My ad ran* Clear Thinking Seminar *with date, venue and content. Clear statements with no ambiguity. The seminar ran with the required numbers. I had learned my lesson.*

The second story I will share with you involves the 'European Commission' a very prestigious body that governs all within the European Union. I have been told (by very reliable sources) that one of their favourite phrases to use when they have no idea of how to comment on a paper or answer a question is 'I would like to have a scrutiny reservation on that please'. Scrutiny reservation? How wonderful! I wish we could all get away with that one.

Imagine asking for a 'scrutiny reservation' at your next meeting. Apparently, the phrase is so widely used now in the European Commission that people take it quite seriously as being very meaningful. I rest my case.

QUICK
THINKING

Remember WHAT to do

☺ Always check for clarity

☺ Ask for meaning

☺ Question meaning

☺ Avoid jargon

☺ Ask them to 'say it another way'

8
CREATING THE DILEMMA

> *In my experience you pay for what you don't like beforehand, and you pay for what you do like, afterwards*

WHAT IT IS

The trick of 'creating the dilemma' occurs when we are forced to see things as an 'either/or' or a 'black and white' situation. But very few situations in life are this stark. Normally we are faced with many options and challenges, and the point of clear thinking is to see as many possibilities as we can when solving problems and making decisions. In this way, we can make an informed choice.

'Creating the dilemma' is sometimes called 'using the either/or syndrome.' When someone hits you with this, they can do it in two ways: **forcing the issue** and the **illusion of choice**.

HOW IT HAPPENS

Forcing the issue

They hit your emotions. For example, at a meeting, when agreement is being sought and you are asking questions, trying to find out more someone says something like: 'Look, you are wasting time here, you are either with us or against us. Which is it to be?' Thus, forcing you into an extreme position from which you now have to make a choice.

If you fall for this trick, you will want to defend yourself from being against everyone. But you are not against anyone. Your questions are simply asking for clarity and more information. You have nothing to defend. However, you will feel you need to defend yourself if you react emotionally to this trigger.

A very common version of this, which is frequently heard at many business meetings and in lots of disputes and heated discussions, is the phrase: 'are we part of the *problem* or the *solution* here?'

Imagine you are at that meeting. It has gone on a long time. Your boss is trying to achieve a consensus decision and people are discussing things further, asking questions, seeking clarity. He is getting impatient and blurts out this phrase ... 'Look are we part of the problem here or the solution?'

How would you answer? Would you want to reply that you are part of the solution ... of course? Yes, indeed most of us would like to think we are helping in a situation, not hindering it and we would definitely like to be seen in that light. That is why the trick of 'creating the dilemma' is so powerful. There are only two sides – the goodies and the baddies, and the person using it knows we will all want to rush to be the goodies.

Alternatively, even though you want to be a goodie, you might feel accused of being one of the baddies and respond with something like 'You think some of us are causing problems here? What exactly do you mean?' This of course is very defensive and will ensure your train of thought will be diverted away from your goal of seeking clarity.

'Creating a dilemma' is a way of defining a situation so that people's thinking will be caught in an either/or trap. 'Either I'm part of the problem here, or the solution', 'I'm either with them or against them'. If this is put to me, I have to make a very limited choice, extremely limited in fact and it is a choice that has been defined for me by the speaker. My thinking is limited to the choices given to me. If I could really think about what is going on I would probably realise that I am against no one, that the situation is not about who is part of a problem or a solution. We are at a meeting looking for clarity, asking questions and seeking information so we can make an informed, broad-minded decision and that takes time.

${\mathcal{A}}$CTIONS YOU TAKE

☞ *Take back the situation and redefine it*
The reason why this trick is so persuasive is that the speaker is able to define how you see the situation. It is black or white, easy – make your choice, they say. But is it?

Redefine it the way you see it. For example, you might say 'I think the situation is more complex than that. This is not an either/or situation. I believe we need to look at all the options'
or
'It's not that I'm for or against anyone, I am just looking for clarity and would like to discuss some of these points with you further, before we make our decision.'

It's a simple trick but never allow your thinking to be rail-roaded into making choices – not until you are ready that is.

${\mathcal{H}}$OW IT HAPPENS

The illusion of choice
The second way to be trapped by the either/or syndrome is when someone hits your intellectual vanity. For example, you

may be discussing a decision to be made. Let's say you are deciding to go out for the evening. Your friend says: 'We have two choices here. We can either go to the theatre or the cinema, which would you prefer?

If you fall for this you will begin to evaluate, judge and compare these choices. What films do you know are on at present, are they good, have you read the reviews, do you agree with them? Then again there are some good plays, how informed are you about these? Do you want to show off your great knowledge? If you do you will have a very intellectual and stimulating discussion with your friend around what is presently at the theatre or cinema and most likely you will end up choosing one or other.

But the point you must remember is that these two choices are the two choices of the speaker – the theatre and the cinema, pre-selected by the speaker as their preferences. So, in choosing one, you are walking into a trap where the selection has been already rigged to the other person's advantage.

You might after all have preferred to go for a meal! But since this choice wasn't given, you are less likely to think of it, because you are so caught up in making a choice between the film and the play. Or perhaps you are simply too polite!

Salespeople are expert at creating this illusion of choice. To close a deal, to get you to reach a decision on buying a product, they will use this trigger. For example if you are choosing to buy a car, they may say something like 'Would you prefer the red one or the green one? Thus, directing your thoughts to decide on *what colour* as opposed to what car?

The choice is a phoney one. You are going to buy a car, there is no choice there, but if you feel you can choose something within that deal it will make you feel freer to make the purchase.

We do this to our children. Have you ever said to your children when trying to get them to bed 'Do you want to go to bed at 7 p.m. or 7.30 p.m.?' What a choice – there is none, they are going to bed ... However, they love it when they think they have an input into that choice.

𝓐CTIONS YOU TAKE

☞ *Ask for more options*

Again, this is very simple. Whenever you are given two options to choose from when making a decision, always simply ask 'Is there a third option?' Or 'Why are there only two choices here – why not more?'

Let them explain their way out of that!

𝓣RUE SUCCESS STORY

In early 1990, John set up in business with his partner Mark producing fun gadget items that sold very successfully in the 'buy for pleasure' market. Five years later, the business had become quite successful and things were running along very smoothly. John and Mark worked well together, they were completely different personalities and this was good for their business. John was the quieter, logical thinker, while Mark was the driven one, always forging ahead with new ideas.

At one particular meeting mid 1995, they began to argue over whether they should take on a new venture. John was hesitant because he felt there was a lot of risk involved with a large capital outlay. Mark was becoming impatient as he felt they could be missing out on an enormous opportunity. Totally exasperated Mark shouted at John, 'Look I know there is a risk in going ahead with this new product. There's a risk that we'll lose money, but there is a risk in everything. There's even a risk in sitting in the garden sunning yourself.'

John was stunned. His thinking for a moment paralysed. He saw that Mark acknowledged there was a risk in losing money, and he did see that yes, there is a risk in almost everything we do in life – and yet we still do it. That is the message Mark was trying to get across. John's thinking began to get caught in the dilemma 'We either take a risk or we don't' and he began to consider maybe they should go ahead as there is a risk in everything. But then he realised his thinking was trapped, set up if you like. He should not be thinking 'Is there a risk or not a risk here?' he should be considering what **degree** of risk there is.

Mark's outburst was forcing him to think in two extremes, either risk or no risk, when in fact he should have been considering a specific type of risk. Once he saw this clarity in his thinking, he said to Mark, 'I understand there is a risk, but the real figures I want to see from you, is what degree of risk we are talking about here. If we can measure the degree of risk we are talking about then we can take an informed decision on whether to go ahead.

Mark was then forced to carry out a proper analysis of the viability of the product. As it happened he did this, with the result that they were able to go ahead with the new product, with both partners more secure and comfortable about the outcome. And yes, though slow to start with, the product became a retail success in the end.

QUICK
THINKING

Summary of WHAT to do

☺ State simply 'this is not an either/or situation'

☺ Take back the situation and redefine it the way you see it

☺ Ask why there are not more than two choices

☺ Ask for a third option

9

FALSE ANALOGY – THE GOOD STORY

My mind works like lightning – one brilliant flash and it's gone

WHAT IT IS

Everyone loves a good story. One of the easiest ways to convince people is to illustrate your point by telling a story or giving an example, comparison or analogy. A good story or analogy will usually have wonderful visualisation and simple, direct language. For example if a teacher is trying to inspire you to use sharply aimed clear thinking when persuading others, they might say 'A carefully aimed pebble can create ripples that spread far and wide'.

This analogy is very simple, with very clear visualisation and can get the message across instantly. But is it actually a true comparison? What have pebbles and clear thought processes got in common you may wonder? Absolutely nothing. So even if a pebble can create ripples that spread far and wide, which really is lovely, I'm afraid that doesn't prove in any way that clear, sharply aimed thoughts will do the same. However, the image of the pebble can perhaps *inspire* you to be just as careful with the aim of your clear thoughts as you would be with your aim when throwing a pebble into the water.

Because of this power of inspiration, you will often hear great speakers with an entire speech of motivational stories, packed with examples and analogies, to inspire their audiences that they too can achieve their goals, no matter how difficult they might think they are. Martin Luther King's wonderful phrase 'I have a dream' inspired millions to fight against prejudice and better their position.

The power of good stories and witty analogies is that they are great tools of communication. We understand instantly what someone is telling us. The immediacy of that understanding is very attractive. We don't have to work it out. It is not difficult for our brain to get around the idea. Also, not only do we understand what is being said, we are being seduced, by the story or analogy, into believing in the point being made.

This is the danger of analogies, stories and examples. If we find them attractive, and if we get caught up in the images and vision of the comparisons we can easily lose our critical thinking faculty to judge the validity of what is being said.

For example, here is an analogy to make us believe that private sector corporations, and especially their top directors, should run free of government interference.

> *When we think of our great athletes, nobody would consider interfering with those runners in a race. In fact, the only way to determine who is the best runner we have is not to interfere with them. The economic race is no different. The only way our most efficient companies can prevail is by not interfering with the participants.*
>
> VINCENT BARRY, *THE CRITICAL EDGE*

In a pre-Enron and WorldCom corporation world, we might have been taken in by this one and believed it. But as we all know letting the directors of such large corporations 'run free' has resulted in huge bankruptcy and enormous loss to the workers in these companies. Letting these participants run free has almost brought down the economy instead of strengthening it.

Notice also that the analogy doesn't prove anything. It just emphasises the point, or as someone once said to me, analogies, good examples and stories do a wonderful job of 'colouring in'. They paint a wonderful picture. They make the point you are trying to make more vivid and colourful. However, the one thing to remember if you are on the receiving end of an analogy is that they are *always* to the advantage of the speaker.

And this, of course, is the reason why analogies, comparisons and great stories can be so dangerous for us when 'thinking on our feet'. We are taken in immediately and are no longer in a position to analyse if what is being said is really true in regard to the subject being discussed.

𝓗OW IT HAPPENS

Firstly, I must point out that not all analogies are false. Not all good stories are misleading. Analogies, stories, examples (and yes, statistics) that compare like with like are one of the best methods of communication. In training and education analogies are one of the most common learning tools and are very effective as memory aids. However, you must be able to analyse when they are this good and not be seduced by false and manipulative instances.

So how do you tell the difference?
The first thing to notice, and I will repeat this again because it is so important, is that analogies, good stories, examples and statistics are always, and I mean always, to the advantage of the speaker. As a speaker, when you want to prove your point you

will always choose an example that strengthens your argument. You would want to be extremely daft, for example, to try to persuade your friend Mary to take up yoga classes with you, by telling her that the last friend who went with you 'dropped dead with exhaustion'. This would make no sense and would frighten your friend away from yoga. What would be a lot more convincing would be to recount the wonderful times other people had when you went together. This will give Mary a wonderful picture of the enjoyment of yoga and will probably entice her to go.

However, the analogy of your past friends enjoying yoga in no way proves that Mary will also enjoy it. One liking yoga doesn't mean the other will. You may be making a false comparison but if Mary enjoys the story you are telling her, she will not notice this and could well be persuaded to join you.

ACTIONS YOU TAKE

☞ *Beware*

The first lesson in dealing with analogies, examples, stories and the like is to be aware and beware. False comparisons, weighted examples and good stories can be the trick you fall for most quickly. However, it is also one of the easiest tricks to spot.

Do you remember Jack's story in the *Welcome* section of this book? Jack was in the middle of a presentation, trying to persuade his boss to develop an executive range of men's shirts and market it aggressively in Europe. His CEO interrupts 'I think it's best to stick with our current design. We tried something like this years ago and it didn't work …' I asked you what you would do then. I hope you can see now that what Jack's

CEO has used here is 'a false analogy'. To compare the market today with the European market of several years ago is a false comparison. Also to compare a company in its present state with what it was several years ago is also a false analogy. Markets and companies move on and at today's rapid rate of change they can become very different very quickly.

☞ *Highlight the false comparison*
If you were Jack, you should see the false analogy immediately for what it is. Your response could then be something like 'I appreciate that a lot of effort went into that particular range of design some years ago and we have learned valuable lessons from it. Today we are in a newer market however, one more interested in our type of design. We ourselves are a different company with sharper designs and better customer connections (thanks mainly to the previous attempt). We are now in a much stronger position and I feel convinced that if we don't strike out and expand now, we will be missing a very easy opportunity to make a very handsome profit. Here are my figures ...'

No surrendering under the false analogy. See it for what it is and either show it as a false comparison, and/or add on to it to strengthen your own point – as you did here with Jack's example. Take the analogy back to strengthen your own argument.

☞ *Hear the real message*
Another way examples and comparisons hit are when you are trying something new. For example, people will often say 'but it will be so difficult for you because no one has done this be-

fore'. Or 'it will be so difficult for you because you are a man, woman, black, white, whatever'.

Again, there is no proof for any of this. All this kind of statement shows is that the speaker doesn't think you can do something, or the speaker doesn't want you to do something – whether it be to leave home, break free, start your own career, set up a business, open a flower shop. However, nothing they say here can prove or disprove your future success or failure.

This used to happen to me a lot when I started my business. Some people didn't think I was going to be able to survive. I was a young woman introducing the teaching of *Clear and Critical Thinking* to a corporate world. I was given all sorts of horror stories about how awful this would be. Each time I heard these stories I remember thinking, 'well, this person does not think I can do this, luckily I know I can.'

I never questioned their right to see the world the way they did, I just felt very lucky I didn't share that view. And of course, success is the best accolade. I can now look back and be very pleased at the successful business that has developed throughout Ireland, UK and Europe.

If this is something you encounter, the best thing to do is not to react but simply hear the real message. The real message is that someone doesn't believe you will achieve what you want. Or they may be fearful for your safety in taking such a risk.

You can deal with that. Other people's perceptions or fears shouldn't stop you. You don't have to prove yourself *through argument*. Getting what you want will be your real proof of success. And believe me, these people will be the first to tell you 'I always said you would succeed' when you do.

Remember, there is only one way you can predict the future and that is to invent it.

When someone is trying to convince you with a good story, analogy, example or statistics, just ask yourself 'is this a true comparison?' or 'does this story really make sense? I know it sounds great, but is it able to prove what the speaker is saying?'

Keep a clear head when confronted with this type of thinking. Analyse what is being said to see if it makes any sense. Enjoy a good story if you want to, just don't be taken in by it.

$\mathcal{T}$RUE SUCCESS STORY

This is a story told to me by a delegate at a recent seminar. It is more a warning story, than a story of success, but I believe it is very relevant to this particular trick of manipulation.

A very successful motivational speaker was on radio one evening delivering a wonderful inspirational speech. It was a recording of a recent speech given in a European capital city and was being broadcast by the BBC. The theme of the talk was 'Never give up on your dreams'. The speaker was instilling belief in his listeners by giving a series of stories and examples, with great metaphorical analogies (like the one above about the pebble). People were being seduced to think that because they heard a story of someone else overcoming great difficulties to become successful and reach their dream, the members of the audience could do the same. They were told, for example, that a man who had been in an horrific accident and was told he could never walk again, after great effort and struggle, did walk. And there were further stories on people who overcame poverty and hardship to become rich and famous.

The speaker gave no logical evidence to show that members of the audience were comparable to these people in the stories. No evidence was shown that they would have the same characteristics of courage, strength and tenacity for example. But with good stories and analogies, evidence isn't necessary. The audience is motivated to act when they hear these stories – that is the power of the pictures they paint. If you believe in the story you will be motivated to do what you always wanted to do, but didn't think possible.

This is all very fine if your dreams are good and wholesome. The danger of good stories and analogies is that you may be comparing the heroism of these stories to your own dreams, and therefore making your own dreams heroic – even if they are not. What if, for example, your dream was to shoot your neighbour? This type of motivational speech to go out and actually do it may fire you up. This is very dangerous indeed. Motivational speeches can do the same job of motivating bad people as well as good people. Their danger is in giving credence to insane as well as sane ideas, because nobody questions the ideas themselves. They simply try to make them seem good by comparing them to good things.

For example, in the telling of the same story, or analogy of heroism, a terrorist intent on killing thousands of people will hear his dream just as equally justified as the doctor who is inspired to work diligently to save those same people's lives.

This flaw was pointed out to our motivational speaker on the BBC shortly after the transmission of his talk. Several people phoned in to ask him to clarify how important it is to be clear that the dreams we have are worthy ones, before we embark on convincing ourselves through motivational inspiration to try to achieve them. He agreed this is most important.

QUICK THINKING

Remember WHAT to do

☺ Be aware and beware

☺ Highlight the false comparison

☺ Hear the real message

10
REPETITION

> *It's not that I'm jealous, I just don't like her talking to other men*

WHAT IT IS

As in the one-liner above, the trick of 'repetition' is often very infuriating to have to put up with. People will endlessly repeat themselves over and over again, in an attempt to persuade you that they are the good people or that they know what they are talking about.

(I hope you have noticed 'endlessly repeating themselves, over and over again' is a form of repetition!) We do it, as I have done it here, when we want to strengthen our point. However, all we do when we repeat ourselves is to reinforce what we are saying. We do not justify it in any way or give any evidence to prove our point. Even so, the speaker will want you to believe that they have given you a reason for what they have said, like in the above line 'I just don't like her talking to other men' is supposed to prove this man is not jealous'. This is frustrating because as we can see, all he has done is repeat that he is in fact jealous ... While this instance above is quite humorous, 'repetition' can be a very serious form of manipulation. When statements are made again and again in a confident manner without argument or proof, we tend to believe them quite independently of the presence or absence of evidence for their truth. Again, we tend to accept these statements more readily if someone famous or of great celebrity utters them.

ℋOW IT HAPPENS

Supermarkets for some reason have a strange habit of repeating themselves in quite a blatant way, leaving no chance for subtlety. Here are just three examples:

Do not turn upside down

PRINTED ON THE *BOTTOM* OF A BOX OF TIRAMISU DESSERT

Product will be hot after heating

PRINTED ON A BREAD PUDDING

Warning – contains nuts

PRINTED ON A PACKET OF PEANUTS

Or the funniest one of all for stating the obvious is something I saw printed on a helmet-mounted mirror used by US cyclists:

Remember objects in the mirror are actually behind you.

Maybe we are all stupid. But I suppose these give us a good laugh and so redeem themselves somewhat.

The more dangerous ones are when they masquerade as gems of wisdom or advice. For example, think of the phrase 'too much of something is a bad thing'. It is a wise old saying that we all believe in. However, if you analyse it you will find that it is simple repetition, even though it sounds like a wonderful piece of advice.

'Too much' is a quantity that is wrong, it is too much, not ideal, not what we would want. It is therefore not good, and if it is not good, *ergo* it must be bad for us, as it is too much. So now let us repeat the sentence with our new understanding: 'too much of something is a bad thing' (that which is bad is bad). So, this wonderful piece of wisdom is telling us that 'what is bad, is in fact bad'. Fantastic.

Repetitions are good for getting a message across. You will notice that advertising is all about repetition. The more you see a product, the more likely you are to buy it (they call it 'brand awareness'). However, simple repetition does not give you any evidence to believe in the product. The power of suggestion is in the repetition. During elections politicians know this very well. They will try their utmost to put up as many signs with *Vote for Byrne* or *Vote Smith*, for example, as they can. So the more posters you see the more likely the power of repetition will move you towards voting for these people. They do not put policies up on posters, just the words *Vote, Vote, Vote* with their name. Very clever.

Repetition is quite seductive the more dramatic people become. There is a terrific example of this in the film *12 Angry Men* when one jury member tries to prove that a young boy on trial for killing his father actually did it. He says: 'He killed his father. He stabbed him four inches into the chest. He didn't just flick the knife, he plunged it deep into that man's chest. Imagine the anger he must have felt to plunge that knife so deeply.' As he is saying this he is becoming increasingly dramatic, with the result that the other jurors are beginning to believe the boy must have done it. Because of the art of repetition, everyone is concentrating on *how* the boy killed his father, and not *if* he killed his father. This juror is simply repeating in several different ways 'he killed his father', 'he killed his father', 'he killed his father', whereas in fact he should be trying to prove or justify this statement, not simply repeat it as proof.

⅋CTIONS YOU TAKE

This particular trick is a lot less common in discussions and so you may not have to resort to dealing with it. However do look for it all around you, because it tends to be wherever you are making decisions that are sometimes more important for the other person rather than for you.

As for example when you are purchasing products. Sometimes it won't make a great difference what brand you buy, but it will to the person who makes that brand. They may have no livelihood if everyone stops buying their brand, but it wouldn't affect you greatly if they stopped manufacturing, you could simply buy another brand of the same product. Your purchase of their brand is more important to them than to you. And so the endless repetition of seeing their name everywhere ...

Also, it is more important for the person you vote for, that you vote for him/her. You may never see them on your doorstep again after you place your ballot. But if they don't get *your* vote, they may lose their seat, their ambition, their livelihood. And even if they do get in, it may still make no difference to you.

The easy thing to remember with repetition is not to believe in it. Ask for evidence and proof. If a group or organisation claim they are the best, make them prove it, don't let them just repeat it. Don't be taken in by how many times you see their name, or how many famous people buy their product. If they want to sell to you, make sure the product will be effective in satisfying your needs.

If you are in a discussion with someone and they keep repeating how wonderful they are in so many different ways, ask them to prove it by doing something. Actions speak far louder than words.

𝒯RUE SUCCESS STORY

As a social worker, Liz was used to case conferences with other professionals. These meetings usually involved a medic, a psychologist, sometimes the police and others from the caring professions. The purpose of the meeting would be to decide on the proper care for vulnerable members of society, like the young, old or infirm.

One day, the case conference was regarding a twenty-year-old mother who it was feared was incapable of taking care of her very young baby. The baby had some bruises and Liz, as a social worker, felt the baby should be taken into care for its own sake or at least for some time, until they could assess the situation more carefully. She had a real fear that this young mother might damage her baby further.

The meeting consisted of the usual professionals, as well as the young girl and her solicitor. The solicitor began the proceedings. 'We are here today,' she said, 'to come to a decision as to whether my client is a fit mother or not. But what is a fit mother? And what does the word mother actually mean?'

To get her answer she put the word mother up on a flipchart paper and asked all present to describe what words they would put against it. All the people in the room were mothers. They gave glowing terms to the word 'mother': nurturer, companion, nurse, teacher, advisor, and on and on. When she had a chart full of wonderful words describing 'mother', the solicitor slowly looked at all individually in the room, and said 'Are any of you able to live up to this ideal of what a mother is?'

Everyone in the room was transfixed with guilt – no one of course could live up to this perfect description.

The solicitor then argued, 'Well, how then can you expect my client to do so and why are you even considering taking her child from her?'

For a moment, Liz was confused. The simple trick of repeating the description of 'good mother' over and over again had made all present leave the real issue. Their main concern should have been to make a judgement on whether this particular young girl was capable of taking care of her baby, or would she damage the child in some way? They were there to discuss the probability of this damage based on the evidence.

No one was there to discuss the meaning of motherhood. But what a clever solicitor to try to confuse them like that. The horror of it was that she almost succeeded!

Liz, however, recovered her clear thinking and begun to ask leading questions that returned the discussion back to the case in hand.

QUICK
THINKING

Remember
WHAT to do

☺ Have a good laugh if it is obvious, then ignore it or challenge it if you need to

☺ If someone is becoming dramatic to prove a point notice if they are repeating themselves or giving real evidence. Ask them for proof if there is none

☺ Be aware of being bombarded by repetitive information, especially when you are making decisions that have greater consequences for others than for you

☺ Always ask them to prove themselves

Summary of
THE TEN TRICKS

Just to recap on what might happen to you:

❖ Someone attempts to exert a false authority over you

❖ You may feel fearful, uncertain or doubtful (FUD)

❖ Someone is abusive towards you

❖ They stereotype you

❖ They win an argument, not by proving they are right, but by emphasising how wrong you are

❖ You are accused of having caused problems

❖ The argument sounds great, but you're not sure if the words have any real meaning.

❖ You feel forced into making a choice between two extremes

❖ You are seduced by a great story or brilliant example

❖ You are faced with the repetition of a point, but don't hear any justification for it

THE LAST WORD

So now you know! How are you feeling now that you have all this information? Daunted perhaps? If you are feeling a little perplexed about being able to deal with these tricks now that you know them – don't worry. The most natural reaction to trying to deal with tricks of manipulation is to imagine that you have to deal with them all, at the same time. But that is not so. Most meetings and discussions will run quite smoothly. It is only when you are having difficulty that you will need to be able to understand what is happening at the time. The difficulty will only relate to one or two tricks at a time.

If any one of these situations occur, just think 'false argument', 'trick' or whatever word you need to think of to make you aware that there is a trick being used in the discussion. Do this to avoid the natural response of reacting emotionally to the trick before you know it, and therefore losing your train of thought and direction in the conversation. The main point is to remain calm. Having a key word like 'trick' or 'false argument' or even 'bingo' (you can choose whatever word you wish) grounds your thinking to recognise the manipulation taking place.

Once you are aware there is a trick, you can then choose to exercise a response to the trick in the many ways we have discussed under each chapter heading in this book.

Remember also, that 'quick thinking on your feet' does not mean assertiveness. You may get yourself into more trouble by shouting out in the middle of a conversation, 'false cause', 'FUD', 'mob appeal', etc., as no one will probably know what you are talking about …

Some people, when faced with manipulation, say nothing at all, but keep their strength of mind by understanding what is going on, and by being determined not to be defeated by such manipulation. They do not lose their train of thought, but carry on regardless discussing the core issue in order to reach their goal. You may wish to do this also.

The choice is yours. Each situation you are in will most likely require a different action. Once you are more familiar with spotting these tricks of manipulation you will become more practised at making the correct judgement call concerning your particular response.

To help you on your way let's go straight on to our workshop in Part III. As I mentioned earlier this is a space for you to record and practise your skills. You will have space to:

Clarify your thoughts for what you want before your discussions with others

Note tricks of manipulation that occur at the time

Write your own success stories in order to build up your confidence as you develop your skills.

QUICK
THINKING

PART III

GET GOING ON RESULTS
Your Own Personal Workshop

Introducing your Personal Assistant (PA)

The best way to become expert at 'quick thinking on your feet' is by **practising** these techniques every time you become **aware** of them. Practice and Awareness are the key to success and this workbook is designed to be your unique Personal Assistant (PA) for doing just that.

The workshop begins with a short practice quiz to get you used to recognising the 10 tricks of manipulation. The quiz consists of 10 sample trick statements and asks you to identify which trick each one is. You will be able to test your skills before approaching real life situations and can also enjoy testing family, work colleagues and friends. The rest of the workshop will then concentrate on helping you to use your new skills in real life situations.

High alert thinking

When do we need 'quick thinking on our feet'? It is important to remember, not all the time. You will not need quick thinking on your feet, for example, when you are quite happy and confident doing what you enjoy, happy at your work, at home, or with family and friends. So, please don't think you have to focus on *everything* in your life and perhaps end up frantically analysing far too much.

Quick thinking on your feet will be very helpful to you when you need 'high alert thinking'. That is when you are in a situation that you know needs your best focus and attention, where the consequences may be very serious and important to you. Remember our quick thinking dog story and how he needed to regain all his thought composure to survive ...

In this workshop, we will concentrate on 3 real life situations where high alert thinking is necessary, whether at work or negotiating with family and friends. These situations are:

1   Establishing personal confidence to attain a much-needed goal
2   Working through a challenging one-to-one discussion
3   Delivering your ideas with confidence at meetings.

These three situations cover your ability to think (1) for yourself, (2) on a one-to-one basis and (3) within a large group.

YOUR PURPOSE

This workbook will be a great benefit to you if you approach it with a clear purpose in mind. Remember what I said at the beginning of this book.

'Your purpose may be to change your career, secure a promotion, overcome a phobia, realise a dream, control your wayward teenager... Whatever your purpose, the meaning your bring to it, how you think about it will determine your success. And how you get *others* to think about it will be the key to convincing them to come with you.'

So, remember your purpose when we come to exercising for real life situations. For the moment, let's start with the practice quiz.

PRACTICE QUIZ

Can you name the 10 tricks used below and how would you respond to others saying this to you?

Questions

---

1. We tried that before and it didn't work ...

Name of trick:

What do you do?

---

2. Have you seen the drop in sales since our last price rise? –
I told you it was a bad idea to raise prices this year ...

Name of trick:

What do you do?

---

3. *(Saying to yourself)* **I'll never be able to succeed, I'm just not good enough ...**

Name of trick:

What do you do?

_____

_____

_____

_____

_____

4. We've always done it this way; you're the only one who wants to change around here ...

Name of trick:

What do you do?

_____

_____

_____

_____

_____

5. A colleague of mine has had a bad experience with your product ...

Name of trick:

What do you do?

_____

_____

_____

_____

6. *(At a tense meeting, they say)* **You're either with us or against us ...**

Name of trick:

What do you do?

_____

_____

_____

_____

_____

7. You're pressurising me ...

Name of trick:

What do you do?

_____

_____

_____

_____

_____

8. It's very important to understand that when there's more trade, there's more commerce ...* *[see source on p. 136]*

Name of trick:

What do you do?

_____

_____

_____

_____

_____

9. I've lived amongst them all my life, they're all born liars …

Name of trick:

What do you do?

_____

_____

_____

_____

_____

10. Our competitors will never be able to give you what you want, buy from us …

Name of trick:

What do you do?

_____

_____

_____

_____

_____

This was said by George W. Bush in Quebec City, Canada, 21 April 2001 and I thought you might enjoy it. (Source: Mary, More George W. Bushisms, edited by Jacob Weisberg, Pocket Books, London 2002)

ANSWERS TO PRACTICE QUIZ:

Let's see if you have discovered the trick used in each of these 10 examples and how you responded to it. How do you compare to what you have read in the book? You may have thought of some extra things to say and please keep them in this workbook as future reference for your real life situations.

What is Wrong:	WHAT to do
Use of:	
1. False Analogy (Trick 9)	See pages 109-117
2. False Cause (Trick 6)	See pages 89-93
3. FUD (against self) (Trick 2)	See pages 118-124
4. The Authority Card (Trick 1)	See pages 46-58
5. False Analogy (Trick 9)	See pages 109-117
6. Creating the dilemma (Trick 8)	See pages 102-108
7. Abuse (Trick 3)	See pages 65-71
8. Repetition (Trick 10)	See pages 59-64
9. Stereotyping (Trick 4)	See pages 72-77
10. You're wrong so I'm right (Trick 5)	See pages 78-88

Well, I hope you enjoyed flexing your mental muscles with the warm up quiz. Now let's get on to the real thing.

REAL LIFE SITUATIONS

1. Establishing personal confidence to attain a much-needed goal

QUICK
THINKING

Establishing personal confidence to attain a much-needed goal.

Before convincing others, you need first of all to establish personal confidence in your ability to achieve your goals.

Using the ICTC model (Identify, Clarify, Think and Change) we discussed in Part I, I want you to clarify your thinking to retain the focus for what you want. You need to know:

❖ What you want

❖ What it entails

❖ How you feel about it

❖ How to use your wit to get it

You can do this by working through the following questions.

(A) IDENTIFY your purpose (know what you want)

What is your Purpose ? (write down what you want to achieve, try to make it specific with a time deadline)

_____

_____

_____

_____

_____

_____

_____

_____

_____

Look at it: Is it an 'Ideal' or an 'Idea' (see pages 19, 20)

If it is an ideal (like happiness, wealth, etc.) what **ideas** can you think of to achieve the ideal?

_____

_____

_____

_____

_____

_____

_____

_____

Now look at the number of ideas you have here and choose one you want to make into a true purpose you can work on producing into action.

Take this idea (for example, **I want to get a promotion this year,** or **I want to lose a half stone in 6 weeks**) and gain clarity on *why* you want to do this.

This will give you the confidence to reason it coherently with others.

Ask why 5 times: (see page 20)
What do I want (to do)?

_____

_____

_____

Why?

_____

_____

_____

_____

Why?

_____

_____

_____

_____

Why?

_____

_____

_____

_____

Why?

_____

_____

_____

_____

Why?

_____

_____

_____

_____

Continue asking why until you find you are able to articulate a clear understanding of why your purpose makes good sense. You should then know what you *really* want. This will impress others enormously when you go to persuade them.

So, what is it I really want? *(clarify or repeat as you began)*

_____

_____

_____

_____

_____

_____

_____

_____

_____

_____

THIS IS YOUR PURPOSE and you should now be clear and confident that you know what you want.

You may have found it frustrating trying to answer why 5 times. The less sure you are of your purpose the more difficult it is to delve deeper into clarifying what it is you want. But try to persist, even leaving this exercise for a while and coming back to it in a few days will help you to produce thoughts you may never know existed. And if you find it really difficult to become clear about what it is you want, then perhaps it is a question of do you really want it? Or do you *know* what you want? Think again, maybe you can come up with a new idea – one that suits you better.

Alternatively, you may find you don't have to ask why 5 times, perhaps two or three attempts will yield enough clarity and confidence in defining your goal and your ability to defend it. However, I do advise you to persist as people tend to come up with quite surprising answers as they continue to carry on through the 5 whys.

(B) CLARIFY meaning (know what your goal entails)

Once you have your purpose, the next question is will you succeed or fail in attaining your purpose? Don't confuse your brain by believing you **can't** get what you want, even though you really want it (see page 23).

The answer to your success lies in the **meaning you give to your purpose.** If you don't believe in either yourself or your project then there is every likelihood that no one else will either.

State your purpose (I know, again!)

_____

_____

_____

_____

_____

_____

_____

What meaning are you giving to this purpose, your goal, the thing you want to achieve?

Write down a list of words that give a positive meaning to your goal. For example if I want to go for a promotion, I will write down words that make sense of my understanding to reach for that goal. I will believe that the promotion will be rewarding, interesting, challenging, etc.

Make a list of positive words that give meaning to your purpose:

_____	_____
_____	_____
_____	_____
_____	_____
_____	_____
_____	_____
_____	_____

It is important when you look back on the list of your beliefs about your goal that you can check this against real evidence. Research is always a good move when deciding to change for a better future. If your wish is to move to a new city or new job, check with someone who has been there or done that, because what you believe about your goal, if not checked, may simply be aspirational. And you may get quite a shock when you eventually arrive to find that the job you thought was *so* interesting is in fact boring.

Also, if you have verified that the positive meaning you are giving to your goal is true, then you should be doubly confident that you are doing the right thing.

Now make a list of your positive attributes you have to *achieve* this goal. This should make you feel good and therefore **motivated**, which is essential in gaining confidence to think on your feet. Never forget why you believe you can do what you want to do. Write these attributes down again on a separate page if you like, or photocopy what you have done here. Keep them in a safe place where you can find them when you need to see them. They can be your tower of strength when you go into a difficult meeting or discussion, or when you are having a low moment yourself. Focus and motivation are key measures of success (see page 24).

Believe in yourself

Make a list of all the positive* attributes you have to achieve your purpose, e.g., you are determined, intelligent, have ability …

_____	_____
_____	_____
_____	_____
_____	_____
_____	_____
_____	_____
_____	_____
_____	_____

With positive belief in your goal established, positive belief in yourself is sustainable through your ability to **focus** completely on the goal you want to achieve.

You can do this by looking at how you *feel* about the project you are taking on. Are you passionate or emotional about achieving your goal?

*you may find some negative thinking coming up here when you look at the meaning you give to your goal and your own ability to achieve it. However, we have a separate exercise for negative thinking in part (d) of this section – changing negative thinking into positive action. So for the moment, I would like you to concentrate on documenting the positive only.

(C) THINK with Passion not Emotion

(Know how you feel about your goal)

Are you passionate or emotional about achieving your goal? (to refresh your memory on what this means, see page 28).

To succeed you must always strive to be passionate, that is, your feelings should be focused on achieving your goal and not simply be attached to your *identity* with that achievement.

To clarify this distinction answer the following questions.

What needs to be done to achieve your goal? (list all actions necessary to achieve the desired outcome)

_____

_____

_____

_____

_____

_____

_____

What actions have you taken to ensure you can carry out all of the above?

_____

_____

_____

_____

_____

How will you overcome rejection?

_____

_____

_____

_____

_____

_____

_____

_____

How will you deal with criticism?

_____

_____

_____

_____

_____

_____

If there are insurmountable obstacles what will you do?

_____

_____

_____

_____

_____

_____

_____

What actions are you **not** taking that you should be doing to achieve
your goal?

_____

_____

_____

_____

_____

_____

_____

_____

When are you going to start doing them?

_____

_____

_____

_____

_____

_____

Do you believe you will succeed in this project?

_____

_____

_____

_____

_____

_____

When will that be?

_____

_____

_____

_____

_____

_____

_____

_____

How will you know?

_____

_____

_____

_____

_____

_____

_____

Congratulations. If you have found these questions comfortable to answer then you are passionate about your project. You are focused and determined and will persist towards achievement. If, however, you have some difficulty in answering these questions you may be more emotional about your ego, that is your feelings may be more attached to your *identity* with your project and not the project itself.

It is important to try and shift from being emotional to being passionate, because one of the easiest tricks of manipulation is no. 5 – attacking the ego (or abuse). If you are emotional, you will be a sitting duck for that trick – even if you have a fantastic idea to deliver. Remember, to convince yourself and others, you must focus on the issue, not your ego.

If you are unsure about how you will take criticism or rejection then you are concentrating too much on your own personality. If you are passionate, you will think differently, you will see criticism and rejection as learning tools to improve your thinking. Because when you find out why your goal or project is rejected or criticised it is the first step to improving it.

When you can answer this checklist of questions clearly and succinctly you can be sure you are passionate about your project and not emotional about your ego.

(D) CHANGE Negative Thinking into Positive Action

(Use your wits to get your goal)

The last technique to establish confidence in attaining your goals is the very important ability to change negative thinking into positive action.

Below is the DNA Print (see page 33).

You can use this technique to channel all the negative thinking you have about your goal and your ability to succeed into positive, measurable action.

Using the DNA Print

D – Dream: *Write you Purpose/Goal/Desired Outcome*

_____

_____

_____

_____

_____

_____

_____

N – Negatives: *If this is so great, why are you not doing it? Why don't you have it?*

_____

_____

_____

_____

_____

Keep going, let all the negatives pour out ...

_____

_____

_____

_____

_____

_____

Look at this list of negative reasons. This is extraordinarily valuable information. These negatives are your brain's way of telling you *how* to *get* what you want. It is telling you where to look to overcome the barriers to achieving your goals. By finding answers to the above problematic negative reasons, by being creative in overcoming these barriers you will achieve your goal (see pages 35–39).

Remember: If you have the intelligence to find the problems, you have the intelligence to fix them.

A – Actions: *List all the creative things you can do to overcome the above list of negatives*

_____

_____

_____

_____

_____

_____

Now finish off with an action plan, with time deadline and review date. You may wish to carry out each action separately, or list them as a series of priorities.

Sample

MY ACTION PLAN

To Change Negative Thinking into Positive Action
Actions to do (one only, individually or by priority):

_____

_____

_____

_____

_____

Time deadline:

_____

_____

Review Date:

_____

_____

How will I know I have succeeded?

_____

_____

_____

Now you have clarified your thinking.
You are confident about

>What you want and why
>
>What it entails
>
>How you feel about it
>
>How to use your wits to get it.

You can use these exercises on their own for different occasions or as part of one process to achieve confidence and clarity around one particular issue.

REAL LIFE SITUATIONS

2. One-to-One Discussions

One-to-one discussions are sometimes difficult especially if there are challenging negotiations to be tackled.

PREPARATION AND REVIEW: ONE-TO-ONE DISCUSSIONS

For 'quick thinking on your feet' I have devised some sample questions to help you prepare for a meeting of this kind. These are only sample questions and should be added onto as you gain more experience about your specific situation.

There is also a review section with two options:

❖ **When you get it right**

A review of a successful discussion, where you write your own success story

❖ **When you need to do better**

A review where self-analysis will help you to learn more for future successes.

One-to-One Discussions

Preparation Questions

What do you want to achieve from this discussion?

_____
_____
_____
_____
_____
_____

Who is involved?

_____
_____
_____
_____

Describe the problem situation

_____
_____
_____
_____
_____

What do they believe?

_____
_____
_____
_____
_____

What do you believe?

_____
_____
_____
_____
_____
_____

Is a compromise possible?

_____
_____
_____
_____
_____
_____

If YES: What is it?

_____
_____
_____
_____
_____
_____

If NO: Why not?

_____
_____
_____
_____
_____
_____

Can you think of a new idea that might suit both parties?

_____

_____

_____

_____

_____

What actions will you take to remain focused on achieving your goal
(have passion for your project)?

_____

_____

_____

_____

_____

What will you do to overcome emotional diversions away from your
goal?

_____

_____

_____

_____

What is the best possible question they could ask? You could ask?

_____

_____

_____

_____

_____

What is your answer?

_____
_____
_____
_____
_____
_____
_____

What is the worst possible question they could ask?

_____
_____
_____
_____
_____
_____
_____

What is your answer?

_____
_____
_____
_____
_____
_____

What is your time deadline?

_____
_____

What actions will you require from the other person to know you have been successful?

_____

_____

_____

_____

_____

_____

What can you do to help them?

_____

_____

_____

_____

_____

QUICK
THINKING

One-to-One Discussions

REVIEW: When you get it right

Following a successful discussion do your own WHAT review

Write down how you were successful:

(W) What did you achieve?

_____

_____

_____

_____

(H) How did you achieve it?

_____

_____

_____

_____

_____

_____

_____

(A) Actions you took (summary)

_____

_____

_____

_____

_____

(T) Write your own True Success Story

_____

_____

_____

_____

_____

_____

_____

_____

_____

_____

_____

_____

_____

_____

_____

_____

_____

_____

_____

_____

_____

_____

_____

_____

One-to-One Discussions

REVIEW: When you need to do better

Following a less successful discussion do your own WHAT review

Write down why you feel you were not successful:

(W) What happened?

_____

_____

_____

_____

_____

_____

_____

_____

_____

_____

(H) How did you react? (actual)

_____

_____

_____

_____

_____

_____

_____

_____

Were you Passionate or Emotional?

Illustrate how you were passionate

_____

_____

_____

_____

_____

_____

_____

_____

Illustrate how you were emotional

_____

_____

_____

_____

_____

_____

_____

(H) How would you have liked to react – what *should* you have done? (use your best 'staircase wit' here)

_____

_____

_____

_____

_____

_____

(A) Actions you will take if this happens again

_____

_____

_____

_____

_____

_____

_____

_____

_____

(T) Think about what you have learned – write 3 lessons you will take from this situation

_____

_____

_____

_____

_____

_____

_____

_____

_____

_____

_____

_____

Two further technique to help you analyse this situation to achieve future successful discussions are the DNA print and the '5 whys'.

DNA Print

D – Desired Outcome:

What was to be the desired outcome of your discussion?

_____

_____

_____

_____

_____

_____

_____

N – Negatives:

What stopped you from achieving this outcome?

_____

_____

_____

_____

_____

_____

_____

_____

A – Actions:

What ideas can you think of to overcome these negatives?

_____

_____

_____

_____

_____

_____

_____

_____

_____

Can you action any of this list to improve the situation?

_____

ACTION PLAN

What to Do   **When**
_____

_____

The 5 Whys

The second technique is the '5 whys'. This is not only a good tool for defining purpose, it is also excellent for finding the root cause of problems we encounter during unsuccessful meetings and discussions.

Ask why 5 times:

What is the problem?

_____

_____

_____

_____

_____

Why?

_____

_____

_____

_____

_____

Why?

_____

_____

_____

_____

_____

Why?

_____
_____
_____
_____
_____

Why?

_____
_____
_____
_____
_____

Why?

_____
_____
_____
_____
_____

Clarifying the problem in this way should help you to find a solution.

REAL LIFE SITUATIONS

3. Meetings

Formal or larger group meetings demand a different type of preparation question than one-to-one discussions. However, they will normally have the same problems when reviewing success and failure. For this reason, this section will follow the same format as for one-to-one discussions, but with a different preparation sheet questionnaire.

PREPARATION AND REVIEW: MEETINGS

For 'quick thinking on your feet' I have devised some sample questions to help you prepare for formal meetings. These are only sample questions and should be added onto as you gain more experience about your specific situation.

There is also a review section with two options:

❖ **When you get it right**
A review of a successful meeting, where you write your own success story

❖ **When you need to do more**
A review of a less successful meeting where self-analysis will help you to learn more for future successes.

Meetings

Preparation Questions

Is this meeting necessary? (can we achieve the same aims via phone or email, or from a report?)

_____

_____

_____

_____

_____

What must you do to prepare for this meeting?

_____

_____

_____

_____

_____

_____

Who will attend?

_____

_____

_____

_____

What is the subject for discussion?

_____

_____

_____

_____

Do you have an agenda?

_____

_____

_____

*What is **your** purpose at this meeting?*

_____

_____

_____

_____

_____

_____

_____

_____

Do you have all the information you need to fully understand the subject/ problems to be discussed?

_____

_____

_____

_____

_____

If not, where can you get hold of it?

_____

_____

_____

Do you have the expertise/knowledge required to contribute at this meeting?

_____

_____

_____

If not, where can you source it?

_____

_____

_____

Write down at least 2 main points you wish to make

_____

_____

_____

_____

_____

_____

_____

make sure you say them ...

_____

_____

_____

_____

_____

_____

_____

What actions will you take to remain focused? (have passion for your project)

_____

_____

_____

_____

_____

_____

_____

_____

What will you do to overcome emotional diversions?

_____

_____

_____

_____

_____

_____

_____

What is the best possible question you could ask or be asked?

_____

_____

_____

_____

_____

_____

_____

What is your answer?

_____

_____

_____

_____

_____

What is the worst possible question you could be asked?

_____

_____

_____

_____

_____

_____

What is your answer?

_____

_____

_____

_____

How will you know you have had a successful meeting?

_____

_____

_____

_____

REVIEW: When you get it right

Following a successful meeting do your own WHAT review

Write down how you were successful:

(W) What did you achieve?

_____

_____

_____

_____

_____

_____

_____

_____

_____

(H) How did you achieve it?

_____

_____

_____

_____

_____

_____

_____

_____

_____

_____

(A) Actions you took (summary)

_____
_____
_____
_____
_____

(T) Write your own True Success Story

_____
_____
_____
_____
_____
_____
_____
_____
_____
_____
_____
_____
_____
_____
_____
_____
_____
_____
_____
_____

REVIEW: When you need to do better

Following a less successful meeting do your own WHAT review

Write down why you feel you were not successful:

(W) What happened?

_____

_____

_____

_____

_____

_____

_____

_____

_____

(H) How did you react? (actual)

_____

_____

_____

_____

_____

_____

_____

_____

_____

Were you Passionate or Emotional?

Illustrate how you were passionate

_____
_____
_____
_____
_____
_____
_____

Illustrate how you were emotional

_____
_____
_____
_____
_____
_____
_____

(H) How would you have liked to react – what *should* you have done? (use your best 'staircase wit' here)

_____
_____
_____
_____
_____
_____

(A) Actions you will take if this happens again

_____
_____
_____
_____
_____
_____
_____
_____
_____

(T) Think about what you have learned – write 3 lessons you will take from this situation

_____
_____
_____
_____
_____
_____
_____
_____
_____
_____
_____
_____

MORE HELP

Two further technique to help you analyse this situation to achieve future successful discussions are the DNA print and the '5 whys'.

DNA Print

D – Desired Outcome:
What was to be the desired outcome of your discussion?

_____

_____

_____

_____

_____

_____

_____

N – Negatives:
What stopped you from achieving this outcome?

_____

_____

_____

_____

_____

_____

_____

A –Actions:

What ideas can you think of to overcome these negatives?

_____

_____

_____

_____

_____

_____

_____

_____

_____

Can you action any of this list to improve the situation?

_____

ACTION PLAN

What to Do   **When**
_____

The 5 Whys

The second technique is the '5 whys'. This is not only a good tool for defining purpose, it is also excellent for finding the root cause of problems we encounter during unsuccessful meetings and discussions.

Ask why 5 times:

What is the problem?

_____

_____

_____

_____

_____

Why?

_____

_____

_____

_____

_____

Why?

_____

_____

_____

_____

_____

Why?

_____

_____

_____

_____

_____

Why?

_____

_____

_____

_____

Why?

_____

_____

_____

_____

_____

Clarifying the problem in this way should help you to find a
solution.

QUICK
THINKING

THE VERY LAST WORD

I hope you have enjoyed the 'quick thinking on your feet' workshop and that this workbook has been useful for you. I hope you now feel more comfortable to express your thoughts clearly in both small and large groups. May I make the suggestion that you photocopy the review sessions on meetings and discussions *before* you fill them in. Once completed you can keep each review in your newly created 'Accomplished Quick Thinking' file so as to build up a catalogue of successes (and some near misses) you will achieve over time.

Your file of 'True Success Stories' will be the best achievement this book can produce. Don't hide them away. Make sure they are kept safe – or better still send them to me so I can share them with other readers.

My website address is:

www.clearcriticalthinking.com.

Perhaps we can produce a sequel entitled *Quick Thinking on your Feet – practical success stories.*

Whatever you decide to do, I hope that you are satisfied with your skills of quick thinking and that you will have many more success stories to read over with pride and satisfaction.

Recommended Reading

If you have enjoyed this book and would like some further, very interesting and challenging reading, why not search out some of the following titles:

Breton, Philippe, *La Parole Manipulée*, Editions La Decouverte & Syros, Paris 1997

Marinoff, Lou, PhD, *Plato not Prozac*, Quill, New York 2000

Thouless, R. H. & Thouless, C. R., *Straight & Crooked Thinking*, Hodder & Stoughton, London 1930, 1990

Barry, Vincent E., *The Critical Edge, Critical Thinking for Reading & Writing*, Harcourt Brace, USA 1992

Adair, John, *Effective Decision Making*, Pan Books, London 1985

Ditzler, Jinny S., *Your best year yet*, Thorsons, London 1994

Senge, Peter, *The 5th Discipline*, Currency Doubleday, USA 1990

Covey, Stephen R.,*The Seven Habits of Highly Effective People*, Simon & Schuster, London, 1992

My Sincere Thanks

I would like to acknowledge the assistance of some great people who helped me in so many different ways when writing this book.

For the inspiration

Many thanks to my diverse and interesting client companies whose people were so inspiring and enthusiastic about this book. To mention just some of those, many thanks to all at AIB

Group, GlaxoSmithKline, IBM, The Victoria & Albert Museum, The Revenue Commissioners, Irish Life & Permanent, The Law Society (London), Office of Fair Trading (London). Many Irish and UK Public Sector groups and all the terrific women on the women's initiative training programmes at the Kildare County Enterprise Board Ireland, and Kentucky, USA.

The learning
Sincere thanks to David Rice, Killaloe Hedge-School of Writing, Co. Clare, Ireland, whose weekend programme on writing non-fiction was invaluable, and also for the personal time he gave up to teach me specific writing skills for this book.

The editing
A very special thank you to the business journalist Tina Marie O'Neill who gave me invaluable business editing expertise. To Mary Feehan, editor for Mercier Press, who has understood the value of this book from the start, thank you for thinking me through the 'clicking fingers' concept.

The comfort and support
Many thanks to Ashridge Management College for allowing me the comfort of their magnificent setting in the countryside of Hertfordshire to write this book. Also, a special thanks to the wonderful MBA Students I lecture there, for their support and discussions on the content.

And thank you to all my family and friends for their great support and belief in this project.

PRACTICAL ASSISTANCE AND FOLLOW-UP

Valerie Pierce is an international training consultant who delivers training programmes on the topic of 'Clear & Critical Thinking'. Her courses run throughout Ireland, UK, Europe and the United States.

For further information, see her website at
www.clearcriticalthinking.com

Valerie would be delighted to hear of your experiences and success stories of 'quick thinking on your feet'. Please contact her through her website.